It all begins with a letter.

is for Whitman. Penguin Drop Caps is a series of twenty-six collectible hardcover editions of fine works of literature, each featuring on its cover a specially commissioned illustrated letter of the alphabet by type designer Jessica Hische. A collaboration between Jessica Hische and Penguin art director Paul Buckley, whose series design encompasses a rainbow-hued spectrum across all twenty-six books, Penguin Drop Caps debuted with an "A" for Jane Austen's *Pride and Prejudice*, a "B" for Charlotte Brontë's *Jane Eyre*, and a "C" for Willa Cather's *My Ántonia*, and continues with more classics from Penguin. Penguin Drop Caps is a series inspired by typography—its beauty and its power of expression. A drop cap, or an initial cap, is the first letter of a word when designed and set larger than the surrounding text. It is used to introduce a new idea, paragraph, or chapter. We may recognize such elements from books of our childhood, from sacred and historic texts, and from beautiful early editions of classic literature. Whether they appear in illuminated fifteenth-century manuscripts set by scribes or digitally displayed on Jessica Hische's own Daily Drop Cap blog, a drop cap letter impresses upon the reader the arrival of something of which to take note, something unique and special that deserves to be savored. For the book lover, the series is a nod to the tradition of printing and the distribution of ideas, stories, and opinions—ranging from paper to digital media. For the writer and artist, the series pays homage to the significance of composition, texture, and form. With Penguin Drop Caps, we are inspired by the timeless tradition and craft of letters and their endless capacity to communicate.

—E.R.

When Walt Whitman self-published his *Leaves of Grass* in July 1855 it was a slim volume of twelve poems, alarmingly unfamiliar in form, shockingly frank, unabashedly American, and aggressively democratic. At the time, Whitman was a journalist from Long Island, unknown and full of ambition, but Ralph Waldo Emerson immediately proclaimed the book "the most extraordinary piece of wit & wisdom that America has yet contributed" and hailed Whitman as the poet he had long anticipated: "I greet you at the beginning of a great career." Over the next several decades, Whitman revised, expanded, and often republished *Leaves of Grass*; by his "Deathbed Edition" of the book in 1891–1892, he was recognized as one of the most distinctive poetic voices of the modern world. It is a living text—ruminative but never stagnant, always animate in the American mind. In this spirit, *Leaves of Grass and Selected Poems and Prose* brings together the original 1855 edition with beloved poems from across the length of Whitman's career, along with selected prose pieces, all fiercely supporting D. H. Lawrence's view of Whitman "pioneering into the wilderness of unopened life."

PENGUIN BOOKS

LEAVES OF GRASS AND SELECTED POEMS AND PROSE

WALT WHITMAN (1819–1892) was born on Long Island and educated in Brooklyn, New York. He served as a printer's devil, journeyman compositor, and itinerant schoolteacher, edited the *Long Islander*, and in 1846 became editor of *The Brooklyn Eagle*, a position from which he was discharged for political reasons. After a period in New Orleans, considered seminal in shaping his philosophy, he returned to Brooklyn. Although he had earlier affected the mien of a dandy, he now dressed as a "rough," and became prominent among the bohemian element of New York. In 1855 he published *Leaves of Grass*, which he continued to revise and republish over his lifetime. The Civil War found him working as an unofficial nurse to Northern and Southern soldiers in army hospitals in Washington, D.C. After the war he became a clerk in the Indian Bureau of the Department of the Interior, from which he was shortly dismissed by the Secretary on the grounds that *Leaves of Grass* was an immoral book. During his last nineteen years he lived in Camden, New Jersey. Although not previously neglected, he was particularly in the public eye during these years, when such English writers as William Michael Rossetti, A. C. Swinburne, J. A. Symonds, and Robert Louis Stevenson contended that Americans did not fully appreciate him. Among his works are *Drum-Taps* (1865), *Democratic Vistas* and *Passage to India* (1871), and *Specimen Days* (1882).

JESSICA HISCHE is a letterer, illustrator, typographer, and web designer. She currently serves on the Type Directors Club board of directors, has been named a *Forbes Magazine* "30 under 30" in art and design as well as an ADC Young Gun and one of *Print Magazine*'s "New Visual Artists." She has designed for Wes Anderson, *McSweeney's*, Tiffany & Co, Penguin Books, and many others. She resides primarily in San Francisco, occasionally in Brooklyn.

LEAVES *of* GRASS

AND

SELECTED POEMS
and PROSE

WALT WHITMAN

PENGUIN BOOKS

PENGUIN BOOKS
Published by the Penguin Group
Penguin Group (USA) LLC
375 Hudson Street
New York, New York 10014

USA | Canada | UK | Ireland | Australia | New Zealand | India | South Africa | China
penguin.com
A Penguin Random House Company

This selection published in Penguin Books 2014

ISBN 978-0-14-310743-9

Printed in the United States of America
3   5   7   9   10   8   6   4

Cover design by Jessica Hische and Paul Buckley
Interior design by Sabrina Bowers
Set in LinoLetter Std with Archer

CONTENTS

A Note on the Text .... *xiii*

POEMS FROM
LEAVES OF GRASS

1855

Song of Myself 5
A Song for Occupations 85
To Think of Time 99
The Sleepers 109
I Sing the Body Electric 123
Faces 133
Song of the Answerer 139
Europe: The 72d and 73d Years of These States 143
A Boston Ballad 147
There Was a Child Went Forth 151
Who Learns My Lesson Complete? 155
Great Are the Myths 159

1856

Crossing Brooklyn Ferry 167
Spontaneous Me 175

1860

From Pent-Up Aching Rivers 181
Calamus
   In Paths Untrodden 185
   Whoever You Are Holding Me Now in Hand 186
   For You O Democracy 188
   City of Orgies 188
   To a Stranger 189
   Among the Multitude 190
To a Common Prostitute 191
Mannahatta 193

1865–66

Drum-Taps [1865] and Sequel to Drum-Taps [1865–66]
   Vigil Strange I Kept on the Field One Night 197
   The Wound-Dresser 199
   When Lilacs Last in the Dooryard Bloom'd 202

1867

Small the Theme of My Chant 217
A Noiseless Patient Spider 219

1888

As I Sit Writing Here 223

1891

Good-Bye My Fancy! 227

PROSE

Preface to *Leaves of Grass* [1855] 231

From *Specimen Days*

    Down at the Front 259

    A New York Soldier 260

    Abraham Lincoln 261

    Soldiers and Talks 262

    Spiritual Characters Among the Soldiers 264

From *Memoranda During the War*

    Letter to Parents of Erastus Haskell 265

A NOTE ON THE TEXT

In respect to the force of its arrival on the scene, this volume reprints the whole of the initial, 1855 version of *Leaves of Grass* (with titles and section numbers, as they would appear in later editions, supplied in brackets). Added, too, are a handful of poems from across the length of Whitman's career—these taken from the 1891–92 "Deathbed Edition," though arranged chronologically—and selected prose pieces. Interested readers should refer to the Penguin Classics edition of *The Portable Walt Whitman* for an introduction and suggested further reading by Michael Warner, or to *Leaves of Grass: The First (1855) Edition* for an introduction by Malcolm Cowley.

This edition was prepared with the editorial guidance of Peter Coviello, Professor of English at Bowdoin College. He is the author of *Tomorrow's Parties: Sex and the Untimely in Nineteenth-Century America* and *Intimacy in America: Dreams of Affiliation in Antebellum Literature,* and the editor of Walt Whitman's *Memoranda During the War*. He has written as well for venues such as *Raritan, Frieze,* and *The Believer*.

For his editorial work and support on all twenty-six Penguin Drop Caps, thank you to Henry Freedland, who inspired our choice of Whitman for this series.

LEAVES *of* GRASS

AND

SELECTED POEMS *and* PROSE

POEMS FROM
LEAVES OF GRASS

 1855

LEAVES OF GRASS

[Song of Myself]

[1]

I celebrate myself,
And what I assume you shall assume,
For every atom belonging to me as good belongs to you.

I loafe and invite my soul,
I lean and loafe at my ease .... observing a spear of summer
    grass.

[2]

Houses and rooms are full of perfumes .... the shelves are
    crowded with perfumes,
I breathe the fragrance myself, and know it and
    like it,
The distillation would intoxicate me also, but I shall not
    let it.

The atmosphere is not a perfume .... it has no taste of the
    distillation .... it is odorless,
It is for my mouth forever .... I am in love with it,
I will go to the bank by the wood and become undisguised
    and naked,
I am mad for it to be in contact with me.

The smoke of my own breath,
Echoes, ripples, and buzzed whispers . . . . loveroot,
    silkthread, crotch and vine,
My respiration and inspiration . . . . the beating of my
    heart . . . . the passing of blood and air through my
    lungs,
The sniff of green leaves and dry leaves, and of the
    shore and darkcolored sea-rocks, and of hay in the
    barn,
The sound of the belched words of my voice . . . . words
    loosed to the eddies of the wind,
A few light kisses . . . . a few embraces . . . . a reaching around
    of arms,
The play of shine and shade on the trees as the supple
    boughs wag,
The delight alone or in the rush of the streets, or along the
    fields and hillsides,
The feeling of health . . . . the full-noon trill . . . . the song of
    me rising from bed and meeting the sun.

Have you reckoned a thousand acres much? Have you
    reckoned the earth much?
Have you practiced so long to learn to read?
Have you felt so proud to get at the meaning of poems?

Stop this day and night with me and you shall possess the
    origin of all poems,
You shall possess the good of the earth and sun . . . . there are
    millions of suns left,
You shall no longer take things at second or third hand . . . .
    nor look through the eyes of the dead . . . . nor feed on
    the spectres in books,

You shall not look through my eyes either, nor take things
    from me,
You shall listen to all sides and filter them from yourself.

[3]

I have heard what the talkers were talking . . . . the talk of the
    beginning and the end,
But I do not talk of the beginning or the end.

There was never any more inception than there is now,
Nor any more youth or age than there is now;
And will never be any more perfection than there is now,
Nor any more heaven or hell than there is now.

Urge and urge and urge,
Always the procreant urge of the world.

Out of the dimness opposite equals advance . . . . Always
    substance and increase,
Always of knit of identity . . . . always distinction . . . . always a
    breed of life.

To elaborate is no avail . . . . Learned and unlearned feel that
    it is so.

Sure as the most certain sure . . . . plumb in the uprights, well
    entretied, braced in the beams,
Stout as a horse, affectionate, haughty, electrical,
I and this mystery here we stand.

Clear and sweet is my soul . . . . and clear and sweet is all that
    is not my soul.

Lack one lacks both . . . . and the unseen is proved by the
     seen,
Till that becomes unseen and receives proof in its turn.

Showing the best and dividing it from the worst, age vexes
     age,
Knowing the perfect fitness and equanimity of things, while
     they discuss I am silent, and go bathe and admire myself.

Welcome is every organ and attribute of me, and of any man
     hearty and clean,
Not an inch nor a particle of an inch is vile, and none shall
     be less familiar than the rest.

I am satisfied . . . . I see, dance, laugh, sing;
As God comes a loving bedfellow and sleeps at my side all
     night and close on the peep of the day,
And leaves for me baskets covered with white towels bulging
     the house with their plenty,
Shall I postpone my acceptation and realization and scream
     at my eyes,
That they turn from gazing after and down the road,
And forthwith cipher and show me to a cent,
Exactly the contents of one, and exactly the contents of two,
     and which is ahead?

[4]

Trippers and askers surround me,
People I meet . . . . the effect upon me of my early life . . . . of
     the ward and city I live in . . . . of the nation,
The latest news . . . . discoveries, inventions,
     societies . . . . authors old and new,

My dinner, dress, associates, looks, business, compliments,
　　dues,
The real or fancied indifference of some man or woman I love,
The sickness of one of my folks—or of myself . . . . or ill-
　　doing . . . . or loss or lack of money . . . . or depressions or
　　exaltations,
They come to me days and nights and go from me again,
But they are not the Me myself.

Apart from the pulling and hauling stands what I am,
Stands amused, complacent, compassionating, idle, unitary,
Looks down, is erect, bends an arm on an impalpable
　　certain rest,
Looks with its sidecurved head curious what will come
　　next,
Both in and out of the game, and watching and wondering
　　at it.

Backward I see in my own days where I sweated through fog
　　with linguists and contenders,
I have no mockings or arguments . . . . I witness and wait.

[5]

I believe in you my soul . . . . the other I am must not abase
　　itself to you,
And you must not be abased to the other.

Loafe with me on the grass . . . . loose the stop from your
　　throat,
Not words, not music or rhyme I want . . . . not custom or
　　lecture, not even the best,
Only the lull I like, the hum of your valved voice.

I mind how we lay in June, such a transparent summer
    morning;
You settled your head athwart my hips and gently turned
    over upon me,
And parted the shirt from my bosom-bone, and plunged your
    tongue to my barestript heart,
And reached till you felt my beard, and reached till you held
    my feet.

Swiftly arose and spread around me the peace and joy and
    knowledge that pass all the art and argument of the
    earth;
And I know that the hand of God is the elderhand of my
    own,
And I know that the spirit of God is the eldest brother of
    my own,
And that all the men ever born are also my brothers . . . . and
    the women my sisters and lovers,
And that a kelson of the creation is love;
And limitless are leaves stiff or drooping in the fields,
And brown ants in the little wells beneath them,
And mossy scabs of the wormfence, and heaped stones, and
    elder and mullen and pokeweed.

[6]

A child said, What is the grass? fetching it to me with full
    hands;
How could I answer the child? . . . . . . I do not know what it is
    any more than he.

I guess it must be the flag of my disposition, out of hopeful
    green stuff woven.

Or I guess it is the handkerchief of the Lord,
A scented gift and remembrancer designedly dropped,
Bearing the owner's name someway in the corners, that we
    may see and remark, and say Whose?

Or I guess the grass is itself a child . . . . the produced babe of
    the vegetation.

Or I guess it is a uniform hieroglyphic,
And it means, Sprouting alike in broad zones and narrow
    zones,
Growing among black folks as among white,
Kanuck, Tuckahoe, Congressman, Cuff, I give them the same,
    I receive them the same.

And now it seems to me the beautiful uncut hair of graves.

Tenderly will I use you curling grass,
It may be you transpire from the breasts of young men,
It may be if I had known them I would have loved them;
It may be you are from old people and from women, and
    from offspring taken soon out of their mothers' laps,
And here you are the mothers' laps.

This grass is very dark to be from the white heads of old
    mothers,
Darker than the colorless beards of old men,
Dark to come from under the faint red roofs of mouths.

O I perceive after all so many uttering tongues!
And I perceive they do not come from the roofs of mouths
    for nothing.

I wish I could translate the hints about the dead young men
      and women,
And the hints about old men and mothers, and the offspring
      taken soon out of their laps.

What do you think has become of the young and old men?
And what do you think has become of the women and
      children?

They are alive and well somewhere;
The smallest sprout shows there is really no death,
And if ever there was it led forward life, and does not
      wait at the end to arrest it,
And ceased the moment life appeared.

All goes onward and outward .... and nothing collapses,
And to die is different from what any one supposed, and
      luckier.

[7]

Has any one supposed it lucky to be born?
I hasten to inform him or her it is just as lucky to die, and I
      know it.

I pass death with the dying, and birth with the new-washed
      babe. . . . and am not contained between my hat and
      boots,
And peruse manifold objects, no two alike, and every one
      good,
The earth good, and the stars good, and their adjuncts all
      good.

I am not an earth nor an adjunct of an earth,
I am the mate and companion of people, all just as immortal
      and fathomless as myself;
They do not know how immortal, but I know.

Every kind for itself and its own . . . . for me mine male and
      female,
For me all that have been boys and that love women,
For me the man that is proud and feels how it stings to be
      slighted,
For me the sweetheart and the old maid . . . . for me mothers
      and the mothers of mothers,
For me lips that have smiled, eyes that have shed tears,
For me children and the begetters of children.

Who need be afraid of the merge?
Undrape . . . . you are not guilty to me, nor stale nor
      discarded,
I see through the broadcloth and gingham whether
      or no,
And am around, tenacious, acquisitive, tireless . . . . and can
      never be shaken away.

[8]

The little one sleeps in its cradle,
I lift the gauze and look a long time, and silently brush away
      flies with my hand.

The youngster and the redfaced girl turn aside up the bushy
      hill,
I peeringly view them from the top.

The suicide sprawls on the bloody floor of the bedroom,
It is so .... I witnessed the corpse .... there the pistol had
    fallen.

The blab of the pave .... the tires of carts and sluff of
    bootsoles and talk of the promenaders,
The heavy omnibus, the driver with his interrogating thumb,
    the clank of the shod horses on the granite floor,
The carnival of sleighs, the clinking and shouted jokes and
    pelts of snowballs;
The hurrahs for popular favorites .... the fury of roused
    mobs,
The flap of the curtained litter—the sick man inside, borne to
    the hospital,
The meeting of enemies, the sudden oath, the blows
    and fall,
The excited crowd—the policeman with his star quickly
    working his passage to the centre of the crowd;
The impassive stones that receive and return so many
    echoes,
The souls moving along .... are they invisible while the least
    atom of the stones is visible?
What groans of overfed or half-starved who fall on the flags
    sunstruck or in fits,
What exclamations of women taken suddenly, who hurry
    home and give birth to babes,
What living and buried speech is always vibrating here ....
    what howls restrained by decorum,
Arrests of criminals, slights, adulterous offers made,
    acceptances, rejections with convex lips,
I mind them or the resonance of them .... I come again and
    again.

[9]

The big doors of the country-barn stand open and ready,
The dried grass of the harvest-time loads the slow-drawn
    wagon,
The clear light plays on the brown gray and green
    intertinged,
The armfuls are packed to the sagging mow:
I am there . . . . I help . . . . I came stretched atop of the load,
I felt its soft jolts . . . . one leg reclined on the other,
I jump from the crossbeams, and seize the clover and
    timothy,
And roll head over heels, and tangle my hair full of wisps.

[10]

Alone far in the wilds and mountains I hunt,
Wandering amazed at my own lightness and glee,
In the late afternoon choosing a safe spot to pass the night,
Kindling a fire and broiling the freshkilled game,
Soundly falling asleep on the gathered leaves, my dog and
    gun by my side.

The Yankee clipper is under her three skysails . . . . she cuts
    the sparkle and scud,
My eyes settle the land . . . . I bend at her prow or shout
    joyously from the deck.

The boatmen and clamdiggers arose early and stopped for
    me,
I tucked my trowser-ends in my boots and went and had a
    good time,
You should have been with us that day round the chowder-
    kettle.

I saw the marriage of the trapper in the open air in the
    far-west . . . . the bride was a red girl,
Her father and his friends sat near by crosslegged and
    dumbly smoking . . . . they had moccasins to their feet
    and large thick blankets hanging from their shoulders;
On a bank lounged the trapper . . . . he was dressed mostly in
    skins . . . . his luxuriant beard and curls protected his
    neck,
One hand rested on his rifle . . . . the other hand held firmly
    the wrist of the red girl,
She had long eyelashes . . . . her head was bare . . . . her
    coarse straight locks descended upon her voluptuous
    limbs and reached to her feet.

The runaway slave came to my house and stopped outside,
I heard his motions crackling the twigs of the woodpile,
Through the swung half-door of the kitchen I saw him
    limpsey and weak,
And went where he sat on a log, and led him in and assured
    him,
And brought water and filled a tub for his sweated body and
    bruised feet,
And gave him a room that entered from my own, and gave
    him some coarse clean clothes,
And remember perfectly well his revolving eyes and his
    awkwardness,
And remember putting plasters on the galls of his neck and
    ankles;
He staid with me a week before he was recuperated and
    passed north,
I had him sit next me at table . . . . my firelock leaned in the
    corner.

[11]

Twenty-eight young men bathe by the shore,
Twenty-eight young men, and all so friendly,
Twenty-eight years of womanly life, and all so lonesome.

She owns the fine house by the rise of the bank,
She hides handsome and richly drest aft the blinds of the
     window.

Which of the young men does she like the best?
Ah the homeliest of them is beautiful to her.

Where are you off to, lady? for I see you,
You splash in the water there, yet stay stock still in your
     room.

Dancing and laughing along the beach came the twenty-
     ninth bather,
The rest did not see her, but she saw them and loved them.

The beards of the young men glistened with wet, it ran from
     their long hair,
Little streams passed all over their bodies.

An unseen hand also passed over their bodies,
It descended tremblingly from their temples and ribs.

The young men float on their backs, their white bellies swell
     to the sun .... they do not ask who seizes fast to them,
They do not know who puffs and declines with pendant and
     bending arch,
They do not think whom they souse with spray.

[12]

The butcher-boy puts off his killing-clothes, or sharpens his
     knife at the stall in the market,
I loiter enjoying his repartee and his shuffle and breakdown.

Blacksmiths with grimed and hairy chests environ the anvil,
Each has his main-sledge .... they are all out .... there is a
     great heat in the fire.

From the cinder-strewed threshold I follow their movements,
The lithe sheer of their waists plays even with their massive
     arms,
Overhand the hammers roll—overhand so slow—overhand
     so sure,
They do not hasten, each man hits in his place.

[13]

The negro holds firmly the reins of his four horses .... the
     block swags underneath on its tied-over chain,
The negro that drives the huge dray of the
     stoneyard .... steady and tall he stands poised on one
     leg on the stringpiece,
His blue shirt exposes his ample neck and breast and
     loosens over his hipband,
His glance is calm and commanding .... he tosses the slouch
     of his hat away from his forehead,
The sun falls on his crispy hair and moustache .... falls on
     the black of his polish'd and perfect limbs.

I behold the picturesque giant and love him .... and I do not
     stop there,
I go with the team also.

In me the caresser of life wherever moving . . . . backward as
     well as forward slueing,
To niches aside and junior bending.

Oxen that rattle the yoke or halt in the shade, what is that
     you express in your eyes?
It seems to me more than all the print I have read in my life.

My tread scares the wood-drake and wood-duck on my
     distant and daylong ramble,
They rise together, they slowly circle around.
. . . . I believe in those winged purposes,
And acknowledge the red yellow and white playing within
     me,
And consider the green and violet and the tufted crown
     intentional;
And do not call the tortoise unworthy because she is not
     something else,
And the mocking bird in the swamp never studied the gamut,
     yet trills pretty well to me,
And the look of the bay mare shames silliness out of me.

[14]

The wild gander leads his flock through the cool night,
Ya-honk! he says, and sounds it down to me like an
     invitation;
The pert may suppose it meaningless, but I listen closer,
I find its purpose and place up there toward the November
     sky.

The sharphoofed moose of the north, the cat on the
     housesill, the chickadee, the prairie-dog,

The litter of the grunting sow as they tug at her teats,
The brood of the turkeyhen, and she with her halfspread
    wings,
I see in them and myself the same old law.

The press of my foot to the earth springs a hundred
    affections,
They scorn the best I can do to relate them.

I am enamoured of growing outdoors,
Of men that live among cattle or taste of the ocean or woods,
Of the builders and steerers of ships, of the wielders of axes
    and mauls, of the drivers of horses,
I can eat and sleep with them week in and week out.

What is commonest and cheapest and nearest and easiest
    is Me,
Me going in for my chances, spending for vast returns,
Adorning myself to bestow myself on the first that will
    take me,
Not asking the sky to come down to my goodwill,
Scattering it freely forever.

[15]

The pure contralto sings in the organloft,
The carpenter dresses his plank .... the tongue of his
    foreplane whistles its wild ascending lisp,
The married and unmarried children ride home to their
    thanksgiving dinner,
The pilot seizes the king-pin, he heaves down with a
    strong arm,

The mate stands braced in the whaleboat, lance and harpoon
    are ready,

The duck-shooter walks by silent and cautious stretches,

The deacons are ordained with crossed hands at the altar,

The spinning-girl retreats and advances to the hum of the
    big wheel,

The farmer stops by the bars of a Sunday and looks at the
    oats and rye,

The lunatic is carried at last to the asylum a confirmed case,

He will never sleep any more as he did in the cot in his
    mother's bedroom;

The jour printer with gray head and gaunt jaws works at his
    case,

He turns his quid of tobacco, his eyes get blurred with the
    manuscript;

The malformed limbs are tied to the anatomist's table,

What is removed drops horribly in a pail;

The quadroon girl is sold at the stand . . . . the drunkard nods
    by the barroom stove,

The machinist rolls up his sleeves . . . . the policeman travels
    his beat . . . . the gatekeeper marks who pass,

The young fellow drives the express-wagon . . . . I love him
    though I do not know him;

The half-breed straps on his light boots to compete in the
    race,

The western turkey-shooting draws old and young . . . . some
    lean on their rifles, some sit on logs,

Out from the crowd steps the marksman and takes his
    position and levels his piece;

The groups of newly-come immigrants cover the wharf or
    levee,

The woollypates hoe in the sugarfield, the overseer views
    them from his saddle;
The bugle calls in the ballroom, the gentlemen run for their
    partners, the dancers bow to each other;
The youth lies awake in the cedar-roofed garret and harks to
    the musical rain,
The Wolverine sets traps on the creek that helps fill the Huron,
The reformer ascends the platform, he spouts with his
    mouth and nose,
The company returns from its excursion, the darkey brings
    up the rear and bears the well-riddled target,
The squaw wrapt in her yellow-hemmed cloth is offering
    moccasins and beadbags for sale,
The connoisseur peers along the exhibition-gallery with
    halfshut eyes bent sideways,
The deckhands make fast the steamboat, the plank is thrown
    for the shoregoing passengers,
The young sister holds out the skein, the elder sister winds it
    off in a ball and stops now and then for the knots,
The one-year wife is recovering and happy, a week ago she
    bore her first child,
The cleanhaired Yankee girl works with her sewing-machine
    or in the factory or mill,
The nine months' gone is in the parturition chamber, her
    faintness and pains are advancing;
The pavingman leans on his twohanded rammer—the
    reporter's lead flies swiftly over the notebook—the
    signpainter is lettering with red and gold,
The canal-boy trots on the towpath—the bookkeeper counts
    at his desk—the shoemaker waxes his thread,
The conductor beats time for the band and all the
    performers follow him,

The child is baptised—the convert is making the first
    professions,
The regatta is spread on the bay .... how the white sails
    sparkle!
The drover watches his drove, he sings out to them that
    would stray,
The pedlar sweats with his pack on his back—the purchaser
    higgles about the odd cent,
The camera and plate are prepared, the lady must sit for her
    daguerreotype,
The bride unrumples her white dress, the minutehand of the
    clock moves slowly,
The opium eater reclines with rigid head and just-opened
    lips,
The prostitute draggles her shawl, her bonnet bobs on her
    tipsy and pimpled neck,
The crowd laugh at her blackguard oaths, the men jeer and
    wink to each other,
(Miserable! I do not laugh at your oaths nor jeer you,)
The President holds a cabinet council, he is surrounded by
    the great secretaries,
On the piazza walk five friendly matrons with twined arms;
The crew of the fish-smack pack repeated layers of halibut
    in the hold,
The Missourian crosses the plains toting his wares and his
    cattle,
The fare-collector goes through the train—he gives notice by
    the jingling of loose change,
The floormen are laying the floor—the tinners are tinning
    the roof—the masons are calling for mortar,
In single file each shouldering his hod pass onward the
    laborers;

Seasons pursuing each other the indescribable crowd is
gathered . . . . it is the Fourth of July . . . . what salutes of
cannon and small arms!
Seasons pursuing each other the plougher ploughs and the
mower mows and the wintergrain falls in the ground;
Off on the lakes the pikefisher watches and waits by the hole
in the frozen surface,
The stumps stand thick round the clearing, the squatter
strikes deep with his axe,
The flatboatmen make fast toward dusk near the cottonwood
or pekantrees,
The coon-seekers go now through the regions of the Red
river, or through those drained by the Tennessee, or
through those of the Arkansas,
The torches shine in the dark that hangs on the
Chattahoochee or Altamahaw;
Patriarchs sit at supper with sons and grandsons and great
grandsons around them,
In walls of adobie, in canvas tents, rest hunters and trappers
after their day's sport.

The city sleeps and the country sleeps,
The living sleep for their time . . . . the dead sleep for their time,
The old husband sleeps by his wife and the young husband
sleeps by his wife;
And these one and all tend inward to me, and I tend outward
to them,
And such as it is to be of these more or less I am.

[16]

I am of old and young, of the foolish as much as the wise,
Regardless of others, ever regardful of others,

Maternal as well as paternal, a child as well as a man,

Stuffed with the stuff that is coarse, and stuffed with the stuff
    that is fine,

One of the great nations, the nation of many nations—the
    smallest the same and the largest the same,

A southerner soon as a northerner, a planter nonchalant and
    hospitable,

A Yankee bound my own way .... ready for trade .... my
    joints the limberest joints on earth and the sternest
    joints on earth,

A Kentuckian walking the vale of the Elkhorn in my deerskin
    leggings,

A boatman over the lakes or bays or along coasts .... a
    Hoosier, a Badger, a Buckeye,

A Louisianian or Georgian, a poke-easy from sandhills and
    pines,

At home on Canadian snowshoes or up in the bush, or with
    fishermen off Newfoundland,

At home in the fleet of iceboats, sailing with the rest and
    tacking,

At home on the hills of Vermont or in the woods of Maine or
    the Texan ranch,

Comrade of Californians .... comrade of free
    northwesterners, loving their big proportions,

Comrade of raftsmen and coalmen—comrade of all who
    shake hands and welcome to drink and meat;

A learner with the simplest, a teacher of the thoughtfulest,

A novice beginning experient of myriads of seasons,

Of every hue and trade and rank, of every caste and
    religion,

Not merely of the New World but of Africa Europe or
    Asia .... a wandering savage,

A farmer, mechanic, or artist . . . . a gentleman, sailor, lover or
      quaker,
A prisoner, fancy-man, rowdy, lawyer, physician or priest.

I resist anything better than my own diversity,
And breathe the air and leave plenty after me,
And am not stuck up, and am in my place.

The moth and the fisheggs are in their place,
The suns I see and the suns I cannot see are in their place,
The palpable is in its place and the impalpable is in its place.

[17]

These are the thoughts of all men in all ages and lands, they
      are not original with me,
If they are not yours as much as mine they are nothing or
      next to nothing,
If they do not enclose everything they are next to nothing,
If they are not the riddle and the untying of the riddle they
      are nothing,
If they are not just as close as they are distant they are nothing.

This is the grass that grows wherever the land is and the
      water is,
This is the common air that bathes the globe.

This is the breath of laws and songs and behaviour,
This is the tasteless water of souls . . . . this is the true
      sustenance,
It is for the illiterate . . . . it is for the judges of the supreme
      court . . . . it is for the federal capitol and the state
      capitols,

It is for the admirable communes of literary men and
     composers and singers and lecturers and engineers
     and savans,
It is for the endless races of working people and farmers
     and seamen.

[18]

This is the trill of a thousand clear cornets and scream of the
     octave flute and strike of triangles.
I play not a march for victors only . . . . I play great marches
     for conquered and slain persons.

Have you heard that it was good to gain the day?
I also say it is good to fall . . . . battles are lost in the same
     spirit in which they are won.

I sound triumphal drums for the dead . . . . I fling through
     my embouchures the loudest and gayest music to
     them,
Vivas to those who have failed, and to those whose war-
     vessels sank in the sea, and those themselves who sank
     in the sea,
And to all generals that lost engagements, and all overcome
     heroes, and the numberless unknown heroes equal to
     the greatest heroes known.

[19]

This is the meal pleasantly set . . . . this is the meat and drink
     for natural hunger,
It is for the wicked just the same as the righteous . . . . I make
     appointments with all,
I will not have a single person slighted or left away,

The keptwoman and sponger and thief are hereby
    invited . . . . the heavy-lipped slave is invited . . . . the
    venerealee is invited,
There shall be no difference between them and the rest.

This is the press of a bashful hand . . . . this is the float and
    odor of hair,
This is the touch of my lips to yours . . . . this is the murmur
    of yearning,
This is the far-off depth and height reflecting my own face,
This is the thoughtful merge of myself and the outlet
    again.

Do you guess I have some intricate purpose?
Well I have . . . . for the April rain has, and the mica on the
    side of a rock has.

Do you take it I would astonish?
Does the daylight astonish? or the early redstart twittering
    through the woods?
Do I astonish more than they?

This hour I tell things in confidence,
I might not tell everybody but I will tell you.

[20]

Who goes there! hankering, gross, mystical, nude?
How is it I extract strength from the beef I eat?

What is a man anyhow? What am I? and what are you?
All I mark as my own you shall offset it with your own,
Else it were time lost listening to me.

I do not snivel that snivel the world over,
That months are vacuums and the ground but wallow and
    filth,
That life is a suck and a sell, and nothing remains at the end
    but threadbare crape and tears.

Whimpering and truckling fold with powders for
    invalids . . . . conformity goes to the fourth-removed,
I cock my hat as I please indoors or out.

Shall I pray? Shall I venerate and be ceremonious?
I have pried through the strata and analyzed to a hair,
And counselled with doctors and calculated close and found
    no sweeter fat than sticks to my own bones.

In all people I see myself, none more and not one a
    barleycorn less,
And the good or bad I say of myself I say of them.

And I know I am solid and sound,
To me the converging objects of the universe perpetually
    flow,
All are written to me, and I must get what the writing means.

And I know I am deathless,
I know this orbit of mine cannot be swept by a carpenter's
    compass,
I know I shall not pass like a child's carlacue cut with a burnt
    stick at night.

I know I am august,
I do not trouble my spirit to vindicate itself or be understood,

I see that the elementary laws never apologize,
I reckon I behave no prouder than the level I plant my house
    by after all.

I exist as I am, that is enough,
If no other in the world be aware I sit content,
And if each and all be aware I sit content.

One world is aware, and by far the largest to me, and that is
    myself,
And whether I come to my own today or in ten thousand or
    ten million years,
I can cheerfully take it now, or with equal cheerfulness
    I can wait.

My foothold is tenoned and mortised in granite,
I laugh at what you call dissolution,
And I know the amplitude of time.

[21]

I am the poet of the body,
And I am the poet of the soul.

The pleasures of heaven are with me, and the pains of hell
    are with me,
The first I graft and increase upon myself . . . . the latter I
    translate into a new tongue.

I am the poet of the woman the same as the man,
And I say it is as great to be a woman as to be a man,
And I say there is nothing greater than the mother of men.

I chant a new chant of dilation or pride,
We have had ducking and deprecating about enough,
I show that size is only development.

Have you outstript the rest? Are you the President?
It is a trifle . . . . they will more than arrive there every
        one, and still pass on.

I am he that walks with the tender and growing night;
I call to the earth and sea half-held by the night.

Press close barebosomed night! Press close magnetic
        nourishing night!
Night of south winds! Night of the large few stars!
Still nodding night! Mad naked summer night!

Smile O voluptuous coolbreathed earth!
Earth of the slumbering and liquid trees!
Earth of departed sunset! Earth of the mountains
        misty-topt!
Earth of the vitreous pour of the full moon just tinged with
        blue!
Earth of shine and dark mottling the tide of the river!
Earth of the limpid gray of clouds brighter and clearer for
        my sake!
Far-swooping elbowed earth! Rich apple-blossomed earth!
Smile, for your lover comes!

Prodigal! you have given me love! . . . . therefore I to you
        give love!
O unspeakable passionate love!

Thruster holding me tight and that I hold tight!
We hurt each other as the bridegroom and the bride hurt
    each other.

[22]

You sea! I resign myself to you also .... I guess what you mean,
I behold from the beach your crooked inviting fingers,
I believe you refuse to go back without feeling of me;
We must have a turn together .... I undress .... hurry me
    out of sight of the land,
Cushion me soft .... rock me in billowy drowse,
Dash me with amorous wet .... I can repay you.

Sea of stretched ground-swells!
Sea breathing broad and convulsive breaths!
Sea of the brine of life! Sea of unshovelled and always-ready
    graves!
Howler and scooper of storms! Capricious and dainty sea!
I am integral with you .... I too am of one phase and of all
    phases.

Partaker of influx and efflux .... extoller of hate and
    conciliation,
Extoller of amies and those that sleep in each others' arms.

I am he attesting sympathy;
Shall I make my list of things in the house and skip the
    house that supports them?

I am the poet of commonsense and of the demonstrable and
    of immortality;

And am not the poet of goodness only .... I do not decline to
be the poet of wickedness also.

Washes and razors for foofoos .... for me freckles and a
bristling beard.

What blurt is it about virtue and about vice?
Evil propels me, and reform of evil propels me .... I stand
indifferent,
My gait is no faultfinder's or rejecter's gait,
I moisten the roots of all that has grown.

Did you fear some scrofula out of the unflagging pregnancy?
Did you guess the celestial laws are yet to be worked over
and rectified?

I step up to say that what we do is right and what we affirm
is right .... and some is only the ore of right,
Witnesses of us .... one side a balance and the antipodal
side a balance,
Soft doctrine as steady help as stable doctrine,
Thoughts and deeds of the present our rouse and early
start.

This minute that comes to me over the past decillions,
There is no better than it and now.

What behaved well in the past or behaves well today is not
such a wonder,
The wonder is always and always how there can be a mean
man or an infidel.

[23]

Endless unfolding of words of ages!
And mine a word of the modern .... a word en masse.

A word of the faith that never balks,
One time as good as another time .... here or henceforward
     it is all the same to me.

A word of reality .... materialism first and last imbuing.

Hurrah for positive science! Long live exact demonstration!
Fetch stonecrop and mix it with cedar and branches of
     lilac;
This is the lexicographer or chemist .... this made a
     grammar of the old cartouches,
These mariners put the ship through dangerous unknown
     seas,
This is the geologist, and this works with the scalpel, and this
     is a mathematician.

Gentlemen I receive you, and attach and clasp hands with
     you,
The facts are useful and real .... they are not my dwelling ....
     I enter by them to an area of the dwelling.

I am less the reminder of property or qualities, and more the
     reminder of life,
And go on the square for my own sake and for other's sake,
And make short account of neuters and geldings, and favor
     men and women fully equipped,
And beat the gong of revolt, and stop with fugitives and them
     that plot and conspire.

[24]

Walt Whitman, an American, one of the roughs, a kosmos,

Disorderly fleshy and sensual . . . . eating drinking and
    breeding,

No sentimentalist . . . . no stander above men and women
    or apart from them . . . . no more modest than
    immodest.

Unscrew the locks from the doors!

Unscrew the doors themselves from their jambs!

Whoever degrades another degrades me . . . . and whatever is
    done or said returns at last to me,

And whatever I do or say I also return.

Through me the afflatus surging and surging . . . . through me
    the current and index.

I speak the password primeval . . . . I give the sign of
    democracy;

By God! I will accept nothing which all cannot have their
    counterpart of on the same terms.

Through me many long dumb voices,

Voices of the interminable generations of slaves,

Voices of prostitutes and of deformed persons,

Voices of the diseased and despairing, and of thieves and
    dwarfs,

Voices of cycles of preparation and accretion,

And of the threads that connect the stars—and of wombs,
    and of the fatherstuff,

And of the rights of them the others are down upon,

Of the trivial and flat and foolish and despised,
Of fog in the air and beetles rolling balls of dung.

Through me forbidden voices,
Voices of sexes and lusts . . . . voices veiled, and I remove the
     veil,
Voices indecent by me clarified and transfigured.

I do not press my finger across my mouth,
I keep as delicate around the bowels as around the head and
     heart,
Copulation is no more rank to me than death is.

I believe in the flesh and the appetites,
Seeing hearing and feeling are miracles, and each part and
     tag of me is a miracle.

Divine am I inside and out, and I make holy whatever I touch
     or am touched from;
The scent of these arm-pits is aroma finer than prayer,
This head is more than churches or bibles or creeds.

If I worship any particular thing it shall be some of the
     spread of my body;
Translucent mould of me it shall be you,
Shaded ledges and rests, firm masculine coulter, it shall
     be you,
Whatever goes to the tilth of me it shall be you,
You my rich blood, your milky stream pale strippings of
     my life;
Breast that presses against other breasts it shall be you,
My brain it shall be your occult convolutions,

Root of washed sweet-flag, timorous pond-snipe, nest of
    guarded duplicate eggs, it shall be you,
Mixed tussled hay of head and beard and brawn it shall be you,
Trickling sap of maple, fibre of manly wheat, it shall be you;
Sun so generous it shall be you,
Vapors lighting and shading my face it shall be you,
You sweaty brooks and dews it shall be you,
Winds whose soft-tickling genitals rub against me it shall
    be you,
Broad muscular fields, branches of liveoak, loving lounger in
    my winding paths, it shall be you,
Hands I have taken, face I have kissed, mortal I have ever
    touched, it shall be you.

I dote on myself . . . . there is that lot of me, and all so luscious,
Each moment and whatever happens thrills me with joy.

I cannot tell how my ankles bend . . . . nor whence the cause
    of my faintest wish,
Nor the cause of the friendship I emit . . . . nor the cause of
    the friendship I take again.

To walk up my stoop is unaccountable . . . . I pause to
    consider if it really be,
That I eat and drink is spectacle enough for the great
    authors and schools,
A morning-glory at my window satisfies me more than the
    metaphysics of books.

To behold the daybreak!
The little light fades the immense and diaphanous shadows,
The air tastes good to my palate.

Hefts of the moving world at innocent gambols, silently
    rising, freshly exuding,
Scooting obliquely high and low.

Something I cannot see puts upward libidinous prongs,
Seas of bright juice suffuse heaven.

The earth by the sky staid with . . . . the daily close of their
    junction,
The heaved challenge from the east that moment over my head,
The mocking taunt, See then whether you shall be master!

[25]

Dazzling and tremendous how quick the sunrise would
    kill me,
If I could not now and always send sunrise out of me.

We also ascend dazzling and tremendous as the sun,
We found our own my soul in the calm and cool of the
    daybreak.

My voice goes after what my eyes cannot reach,
With the twirl of my tongue I encompass worlds and volumes
    of worlds.

Speech is the twin of my vision . . . . it is unequal to measure
    itself.

It provokes me forever,
It says sarcastically, Walt, you understand enough . . . . why
    don't you let it out then?

Come now I will not be tantalized .... you conceive too much
   of articulation.

Do you not know how the buds beneath are folded?
Waiting in gloom protected by frost,
The dirt receding before my prophetical screams,
I underlying causes to balance them at last,
My knowledge my live parts .... it keeping tally with the
   meaning of things,
Happiness .... which whoever hears me let him or her set
   out in search of this day.

My final merit I refuse you .... I refuse putting from me the
   best I am.

Encompass worlds but never try to encompass me,
I crowd your noisiest talk by looking toward you.

Writing and talk do not prove me,
I carry the plenum of proof and every thing else in my
   face,
With the hush of my lips I confound the topmost skeptic.

[26]

I think I will do nothing for a long time but listen,
And accrue what I hear into myself .... and let sounds
   contribute toward me.

I hear the bravuras of birds .... the bustle of growing
   wheat .... gossip of flames .... clack of sticks cooking
   my meals.

I hear the sound of the human voice . . . . a sound I love,
I hear all sounds as they are tuned to their uses . . . . sounds
　　　of the city and sounds out of the city . . . . sounds of the
　　　day and night;
Talkative young ones to those that like them . . . . the
　　　recitative of fish-pedlars and fruit-pedlars . . . . the loud
　　　laugh of workpeople at their meals,
The angry base of disjointed friendship . . . . the faint tones of
　　　the sick,
The judge with hands tight to the desk, his shaky lips
　　　pronouncing a death-sentence,
The heave'e'yo of stevedores unlading ships by the
　　　wharves . . . . the refrain of the anchor-lifters;
The ring of alarm-bells . . . . the cry of fire . . . . the whirr of
　　　swift-streaking engines and hose-carts with premonitory
　　　tinkles and colored lights,
The steam-whistle . . . . the solid roll of the train of
　　　approaching cars;
The slow-march played at night at the head of the
　　　association,
They go to guard some corpse . . . . the flag-tops are draped
　　　with black muslin.

I hear the violincello or man's heart complaint,
And hear the keyed cornet or else the echo of sunset.

I hear the chorus . . . . it is a grand-opera . . . . this indeed
　　　is music!

A tenor large and fresh as the creation fills me,
The orbic flex of his mouth is pouring and filling
　　　me full.

I hear the trained soprano . . . . she convulses me like the
    climax of my love-grip;
The orchestra whirls me wider than Uranus flies,
It wrenches unnamable ardors from my breast,
It throbs me to gulps of the farthest down horror,
It sails me . . . . I dab with bare feet . . . . they are licked by the
    indolent waves,
I am exposed . . . . cut by bitter and poisoned hail,
Steeped amid honeyed morphine . . . . my windpipe squeezed
    in the fakes of death,
Let up again to feel the puzzle of puzzles,
And that we call Being.

[27]
To be in any form, what is that?
If nothing lay more developed the quahaug and its callous
    shell were enough.

Mine is no callous shell,
I have instant conductors all over me whether I pass or stop,
They seize every object and lead it harmlessly through me.

I merely stir, press, feel with my fingers, and am happy,
To touch my person to some one else's is about as much as I
    can stand.

[28]
Is this then a touch? . . . . quivering me to a new identity,
Flames and ether making a rush for my veins,
Treacherous tip of me reaching and crowding to help them,
My flesh and blood playing out lightning, to strike what is
    hardly different from myself,

On all sides prurient provokers stiffening my limbs,
Straining the udder of my heart for its withheld drip,
Behaving licentious toward me, taking no denial,
Depriving me of my best as for a purpose,
Unbuttoning my clothes and holding me by the bare
    waist,
Deluding my confusion with the calm of the sunlight and
    pasture fields,
Immodestly sliding the fellow-senses away,
They bribed to swap off with touch, and go and graze at the
    edges of me,
No consideration, no regard for my draining strength or my
    anger,
Fetching the rest of the herd around to enjoy them
    awhile,
Then all uniting to stand on a headland and worry me.

The sentries desert every other part of me,
They have left me helpless to a red marauder,
They all come to the headland to witness and assist
    against me.

I am given up by traitors;
I talk wildly . . . . I have lost my wits . . . . I and nobody else
    am the greatest traitor,
I went myself first to the headland . . . . my own hands
    carried me there.

You villain touch! what are you doing? . . . . my breath is tight
    in its throat;
Unclench your floodgates! you are too much for me.

[29]

Blind loving wrestling touch! Sheathed hooded sharptoothed
    touch!
Did it make you ache so leaving me?

Parting tracked by arriving . . . . perpetual payment of the
    perpetual loan,
Rich showering rain, and recompense richer afterward.

Sprouts take and accumulate . . . . stand by the curb prolific
    and vital,
Landscapes projected masculine full-sized and golden.

[30]

All truths wait in all things,
They neither hasten their own delivery nor resist it,
They do not need the obstetric forceps of the surgeon,
The insignificant is as big to me as any,
What is less or more than a touch?

Logic and sermons never convince,
The damp of the night drives deeper into my soul.

Only what proves itself to every man and woman is so,
Only what nobody denies is so.

A minute and a drop of me settle my brain;
I believe the soggy clods shall become lovers and lamps,
And a compend of compends is the meat of a man or woman,
And a summit and flower there is the feeling they have for
    each other,

And they are to branch boundlessly out of that lesson until it
    becomes omnific,
And until every one shall delight us, and we them.

[31]

I believe a leaf of grass is no less than the journeywork of
    the stars,
And the pismire is equally perfect, and a grain of sand, and
    the egg of the wren,
And the tree-toad is a chef-d'œuvre for the highest,
And the running blackberry would adorn the parlors of
    heaven,
And the narrowest hinge in my hand puts to scorn all
    machinery,
And the cow crunching with depressed head surpasses any
    statue,
And a mouse is miracle enough to stagger sextillions of infidels,
And I could come every afternoon of my life to look at the
    farmer's girl boiling her iron tea-kettle and baking
    shortcake.

I find I incorporate gneiss and coal and long-threaded moss
    and fruits and grains and esculent roots,
And am stucco'd with quadrupeds and birds all over,
And have distanced what is behind me for good reasons,
And call any thing close again when I desire it.

In vain the speeding or shyness,
In vain the plutonic rocks send their old heat against my
    approach,
In vain the mastodon retreats beneath its own powdered
    bones,

In vain objects stand leagues off and assume manifold
    shapes,
In vain the ocean settling in hollows and the great monsters
    lying low,
In vain the buzzard houses herself with the sky,
In vain the snake slides through the creepers and logs,
In vain the elk takes to the inner passes of the woods,
In vain the razorbilled auk sails far north to Labrador,
I follow quickly . . . . I ascend to the nest in the fissure of the
    cliff.

[32]

I think I could turn and live awhile with the animals . . . . they
    are so placid and self-contained,
I stand and look at them sometimes half the day long.

They do not sweat and whine about their condition,
They do not lie awake in the dark and weep for their sins,
They do not make me sick discussing their duty to God,
Not one is dissatisfied . . . . not one is demented with the
    mania of owning things,
Not one kneels to another nor to his kind that lived
    thousands of years ago,
Not one is respectable or industrious over the whole earth.

So they show their relations to me and I accept them;
They bring me tokens of myself . . . . they evince them plainly
    in their possession.

I do not know where they got those tokens,
I must have passed that way untold times ago and
    negligently dropt them,

Myself moving forward then and now and forever,
Gathering and showing more always and with velocity,
Infinite and omnigenous and the like of these among
    them;
Not too exclusive toward the reachers of my remembrancers,
Picking out here one that shall be my amie,
Choosing to go with him on brotherly terms.

A gigantic beauty of a stallion, fresh and responsive to my
    caresses,
Head high in the forehead and wide between the ears,
Limbs glossy and supple, tail dusting the ground,
Eyes well apart and full of sparkling wickedness .... ears
    finely cut and flexibly moving.

His nostrils dilate .... my heels embrace him .... his well
    built limbs tremble with pleasure .... we speed around
    and return.

I but use you a moment and then I resign you stallion ....
    and do not need your paces, and outgallop them,
And myself as I stand or sit pass faster than you.

[33]

Swift wind! Space! My Soul! Now I know it is true what I
    guessed at;
What I guessed when I loafed on the grass,
What I guessed while I lay alone in my bed .... and again as I
    walked the beach under the paling stars of the morning.

My ties and ballasts leave me .... I travel .... I sail .... my
    elbows rest in the sea-gaps,

I skirt the sierras . . . . my palms cover continents,
I am afoot with my vision.

By the city's quadrangular houses . . . . in log-huts, or
    camping with lumbermen,
Along the ruts of the turnpike . . . . along the dry gulch and
    rivulet bed,
Hoeing my onion-patch, and rows of carrots and
    parsnips . . . . crossing savannas . . . . trailing in forests,
Prospecting . . . . gold-digging . . . . girdling the trees of a new
    purchase,
Scorched ankle-deep by the hot sand . . . . hauling my boat
    down the shallow river;
Where the panther walks to and fro on a limb
    overhead . . . . where the buck turns furiously at the
    hunter,
Where the rattlesnake suns his flabby length on a
    rock . . . . where the otter is feeding on fish,
Where the alligator in his tough pimples sleeps by the bayou,
Where the black bear is searching for roots or
    honey . . . . where the beaver pats the mud with his
    paddle-tail;
Over the growing sugar . . . . over the cottonplant . . . . over the
    rice in its low moist field;
Over the sharp-peaked farmhouse with its scalloped scum
    and slender shoots from the gutters;
Over the western persimmon . . . . over the longleaved corn
    and the delicate blue-flowered flax;
Over the white and brown buckwheat, a hummer and a
    buzzer there with the rest,
Over the dusky green of the rye as it ripples and shades in
    the breeze;

Scaling mountains . . . . pulling myself cautiously
    up . . . . holding on by low scragged limbs,
Walking the path worn in the grass and beat through the
    leaves of the brush;
Where the quail is whistling betwixt the woods and the
    wheatlot,
Where the bat flies in the July eve . . . . where the great
    goldbug drops through the dark;
Where the flails keep time on the barn floor,
Where the brook puts out of the roots of the old tree and
    flows to the meadow,
Where cattle stand and shake away flies with the tremulous
    shuddering of their hides,
Where the cheese-cloth hangs in the kitchen, and andirons
    straddle the hearth-slab, and cobwebs fall in festoons
    from the rafters;
Where triphammers crash . . . . where the press is whirling
    its cylinders;
Wherever the human heart beats with terrible throes out of
    its ribs;
Where the pear-shaped balloon is floating aloft . . . . floating
    in it myself and looking composedly down;
Where the life-car is drawn on the slipnoose . . . . where the
    heat hatches pale-green eggs in the dented sand,
Where the she-whale swims with her calves and never
    forsakes them,
Where the steamship trails hindways its long pennant of
    smoke,
Where the ground-shark's fin cuts like a black chip out of
    the water,
Where the half-burned brig is riding on unknown currents,

Where shells grow to her slimy deck, and the dead are
     corrupting below;
Where the striped and starred flag is borne at the head of
     the regiments;
Approaching Manhattan, up by the long-stretching island,
Under Niagara, the cataract falling like a veil over my
     countenance;
Upon a door-step .... upon the horse-block of hard wood
     outside,
Upon the race-course, or enjoying pic-nics or jigs or a good
     game of base-ball,
At he-festivals with blackguard jibes and ironical license and
     bull-dances and drinking and laughter,
At the cider-mill, tasting the sweet of the brown sqush ....
     sucking the juice through a straw,
At apple-peelings, wanting kisses for all the red fruit I find,
At musters and beach-parties and friendly bees and
     huskings and house-raisings;
Where the mockingbird sounds his delicious gurgles, and
     cackles and screams and weeps,
Where the hay-rick stands in the barnyard, and the dry-
     stalks are scattered, and the brood cow waits in the
     hovel,
Where the bull advances to do his masculine work, and the
     stud to the mare, and the cock is treading the hen,
Where the heifers browse, and the geese nip their food with
     short jerks;
Where the sundown shadows lengthen over the limitless and
     lonesome prairie,
Where the herds of buffalo make a crawling spread of the
     square miles far and near;

Where the hummingbird shimmers . . . . where the neck of
    the longlived swan is curving and winding;

Where the laughing-gull scoots by the slappy shore and
    laughs her near-human laugh;

Where beehives range on a gray bench in the garden
    half-hid by the high weeds;

Where the band-necked partridges roost in a ring on the
    ground with their heads out;

Where burial coaches enter the arched gates of a cemetery;

Where winter wolves bark amid wastes of snow and icicled
    trees;

Where the yellow-crowned heron comes to the edge of the
    marsh at night and feeds upon small crabs;

Where the splash of swimmers and divers cools the warm
    noon;

Where the katydid works her chromatic reed on the walnut-
    tree over the well;

Through patches of citrons and cucumbers with silver-wired
    leaves,

Through the salt-lick or orange glade . . . . or under conical firs;

Through the gymnasium . . . . through the curtained
    saloon . . . . through the office or public hall;

Pleased with the native and pleased with the
    foreign . . . . pleased with the new and old,

Pleased with women, the homely as well as the handsome,

Pleased with the quakeress as she puts off her bonnet and
    talks melodiously,

Pleased with the primitive tunes of the choir of the
    whitewashed church,

Pleased with the earnest words of the sweating Methodist
    preacher, or any preacher . . . . looking seriously at the
    camp-meeting;

Looking in at the shop-windows in Broadway the whole
    forenoon . . . . pressing the flesh of my nose to the thick
    plate-glass,
Wandering the same afternoon with my face turned up to the
    clouds;
My right and left arms round the sides of two friends and I in
    the middle;
Coming home with the bearded and dark-cheeked bush-
    boy . . . . riding behind him at the drape of the day;
Far from the settlements studying the print of animals' feet,
    or the moccasin print;
By the cot in the hospital reaching lemonade to a feverish
    patient,
By the coffined corpse when all is still, examining with a
    candle;
Voyaging to every port to dicker and adventure;
Hurrying with the modern crowd, as eager and fickle
    as any,
Hot toward one I hate, ready in my madness to knife him;
Solitary at midnight in my back yard, my thoughts gone from
    me a long while,
Walking the old hills of Judea with the beautiful gentle god
    by my side;
Speeding through space . . . . speeding through heaven and
    the stars,
Speeding amid the seven satellites and the broad ring and
    the diameter of eighty thousand miles,
Speeding with tailed meteors . . . . throwing fire-balls like the
    rest,
Carrying the crescent child that carries its own full mother in
    its belly:
Storming enjoying planning loving cautioning,

Backing and filling, appearing and disappearing,
I tread day and night such roads.

I visit the orchards of God and look at the spheric product,
And look at quintillions ripened, and look at quintillions
     green.

I fly the flight of the fluid and swallowing soul,
My course runs below the soundings of plummets.

I help myself to material and immaterial,
No guard can shut me off, no law can prevent me.

I anchor my ship for a little while only,
My messengers continually cruise away or bring their
     returns to me.

I go hunting polar furs and the seal . . . . leaping chasms with
     a pike-pointed staff . . . . clinging to topples of brittle and
     blue.

I ascend to the foretruck . . . . I take my place late at night in
     the crow's nest . . . . we sail through the arctic sea . . . . it
     is plenty light enough,
Through the clear atmosphere I stretch around on the
     wonderful beauty,
The enormous masses of ice pass me and I pass
     them . . . . the scenery is plain in all directions,
The white-topped mountains point up in the distance . . . .
     I fling out my fancies toward them;
We are about approaching some great battlefield in which
     we are soon to be engaged,

We pass the colossal outposts of the encampment . . . . we
    pass with still feet and caution;
Or we are entering by the suburbs some vast and ruined
    city . . . . the blocks and fallen architecture more than all
    the living cities of the globe.

I am a free companion . . . . I bivouac by invading watchfires.

I turn the bridegroom out of bed and stay with the bride
    myself,
And tighten her all night to my thighs and lips.

My voice is the wife's voice, the screech by the rail of the
    stairs,
They fetch my man's body up dripping and drowned.

I understand the large hearts of heroes,
The courage of present times and all times;
How the skipper saw the crowded and rudderless wreck of the
    steamship, and death chasing it up and down the storm,
How he knuckled tight and gave not back one inch, and was
    faithful of days and faithful of nights,
And chalked in large letters on a board, Be of good cheer, We
    will not desert you;
How he saved the drifting company at last,
How the lank loose-gowned women looked when boated
    from the side of their prepared graves,
How the silent old-faced infants, and the lifted sick, and the
    sharp-lipped unshaved men;
All this I swallow and it tastes good . . . . I like it well, and it
    becomes mine,
I am the man . . . . I suffered . . . . I was there.

The disdain and calmness of martyrs,
The mother condemned for a witch and burnt with dry wood,
    and her children gazing on;
The hounded slave that flags in the race and leans by the
    fence, blowing and covered with sweat,
The twinges that sting like needles his legs and neck,
The murderous buckshot and the bullets,
All these I feel or am.

I am the hounded slave . . . . I wince at the bite of the dogs,
Hell and despair are upon me . . . . crack and again crack the
    marksmen,
I clutch the rails of the fence . . . . my gore dribs thinned with
    the ooze of my skin,
I fall on the weeds and stones,
The riders spur their unwilling horses and haul close,
They taunt my dizzy ears . . . . they beat me violently over the
    head with their whip-stocks.

Agonies are one of my changes of garments;
I do not ask the wounded person how he feels . . . . I myself
    become the wounded person,
My hurt turns livid upon me as I lean on a cane and observe.

I am the mashed fireman with breastbone
    broken . . . . tumbling walls buried me in their debris,
Heat and smoke I inspired . . . . I heard the yelling shouts of
    my comrades,
I heard the distant click of their picks and shovels;
They have cleared the beams away . . . . they tenderly lift me
    forth.

I lie in the night air in my red shirt . . . . the pervading hush is
    for my sake,
Painless after all I lie, exhausted but not so unhappy,
White and beautiful are the faces around me . . . . the heads
    are bared of their fire-caps,
The kneeling crowd fades with the light of the torches.

Distant and dead resuscitate,
They show as the dial or move as the hands of me . . . . and I
    am the clock myself.

I am an old artillerist, and tell of some fort's
    bombardment . . . . and am there again.

Again the reveille of drummers . . . . again the attacking
    cannon and mortars and howitzers,
Again the attacked send their cannon responsive.

I take part . . . . I see and hear the whole,
The cries and curses and roar . . . . the plaudits for well aimed
    shots,
The ambulanza slowly passing and trailing its red drip,
Workmen searching after damages and to make
    indispensable repairs,
The fall of grenades through the rent roof . . . . the fan-
    shaped explosion,
The whizz of limbs heads stone wood and iron high in the
    air.

Again gurgles the mouth of my dying general . . . . he
    furiously waves with his hand,

He gasps through the clot .... Mind not me .... mind .... the
    entrenchments.

[34]

I tell not the fall of Alamo .... not one escaped to tell the fall
    of Alamo,
The hundred and fifty are dumb yet at Alamo.

Hear now the tale of a jetblack sunrise,
Hear of the murder in cold blood of four hundred and twelve
    young men.

Retreating they had formed in a hollow square with their
    baggage for breastworks,
Nine hundred lives out of the surrounding enemy's nine
    times their number was the price they took in advance,
Their colonel was wounded and their ammunition gone,
They treated for an honorable capitulation, received writing
    and seal, gave up their arms, and marched back
    prisoners of war.

They were the glory of the race of rangers,
Matchless with a horse, a rifle, a song, a supper or a
    courtship,
Large, turbulent, brave, handsome, generous, proud and
    affectionate,
Bearded, sunburnt, dressed in the free costume of hunters,
Not a single one over thirty years of age.

The second Sunday morning they were brought out in squads
    and massacred .... it was beautiful early summer,
The work commenced about five o'clock and was over by eight.

None obeyed the command to kneel,

Some made a mad and helpless rush . . . . some stood stark
     and straight,

A few fell at once, shot in the temple or heart . . . . the living
     and dead lay together,

The maimed and mangled dug in the dirt . . . . the new-
     comers saw them there;

Some half-killed attempted to crawl away,

These were dispatched with bayonets or battered with the
     blunts of muskets;

A youth not seventeen years old seized his assassin till two
     more came to release him,

The three were all torn, and covered with the boy's blood.

At eleven o'clock began the burning of the bodies;

And that is the tale of the murder of the four hundred and
     twelve young men,

And that was a jetblack sunrise.

[35]

Did you read in the seabooks of the oldfashioned frigate-
     fight?

Did you learn who won by the light of the moon and stars?

Our foe was no skulk in his ship, I tell you,

His was the English pluck, and there is no tougher or truer,
     and never was, and never will be;

Along the lowered eve he came, horribly raking us.

We closed with him . . . . the yards entangled . . . . the cannon
     touched,

My captain lashed fast with his own hands.

We had received some eighteen-pound shots under the
water,
On our lower-gun-deck two large pieces had burst at the first
fire, killing all around and blowing up overhead.

Ten o'clock at night, and the full moon shining and the leaks
on the gain, and five feet of water reported,
The master-at-arms loosing the prisoners confined in the
after-hold to give them a chance for themselves.

The transit to and from the magazine was now stopped by
the sentinels,
They saw so many strange faces they did not know whom to
trust.

Our frigate was afire .... the other asked if we demanded
quarters? if our colors were struck and the fighting
done?

I laughed content when I heard the voice of my little captain,
We have not struck, he composedly cried, We have just begun
our part of the fighting.

Only three guns were in use,
One was directed by the captain himself against the enemy's
mainmast,
Two well-served with grape and canister silenced his
musketry and cleared his decks.

The tops alone seconded the fire of this little battery,
especially the maintop,
They all held out bravely during the whole of the action.

Not a moment's cease,
The leaks gained fast on the pumps . . . . the fire eat toward
    the powder-magazine,
One of the pumps was shot away . . . . it was generally
    thought we were sinking.

Serene stood the little captain,
He was not hurried . . . . his voice was neither high nor low,
His eyes gave more light to us than our battle-lanterns.

Toward twelve at night, there in the beams of the moon they
    surrendered to us.

[36]

Stretched and still lay the midnight,
Two great hulls motionless on the breast of the darkness,
Our vessel riddled and slowly sinking . . . . preparations to
    pass to the one we had conquered,
The captain on the quarter deck coldly giving his orders
    through a countenance white as a sheet,
Near by the corpse of the child that served in the cabin,
The dead face of an old salt with long white hair and
    carefully curled whiskers,
The flames spite of all that could be done flickering aloft and
    below,
The husky voices of the two or three officers yet fit for duty,
Formless stacks of bodies and bodies by themselves . . . . dabs
    of flesh upon the masts and spars,
The cut of cordage and dangle of rigging . . . . the slight shock
    of the soothe of waves,
Black and impassive guns, and litter of powder-parcels, and
    the strong scent,

Delicate sniffs of the seabreeze .... smells of sedgy grass
    and fields by the shore .... death-messages given in
    charge to survivors,
The hiss of the surgeon's knife and the gnawing teeth of his
    saw,
The wheeze, the cluck, the swash of falling blood .... the
    short wild scream, the long dull tapering groan,
These so .... these irretrievable.

[37]

O Christ! My fit is mastering me!
What the rebel said gaily adjusting his throat to the rope-
    noose,
What the savage at the stump, his eye-sockets empty, his
    mouth spirting whoops and defiance,
What stills the traveler come to the vault at Mount Vernon,
What sobers the Brooklyn boy as he looks down the shores
    of the Wallabout and remembers the prison ships,
What burnt the gums of the redcoat at Saratoga when he
    surrendered his brigades,
These become mine and me every one, and they are but
    little,
I become as much more as I like.

I become any presence or truth of humanity here,
And see myself in prison shaped like another man,
And feel the dull unintermitted pain.

For me the keepers of convicts shoulder their carbines and
    keep watch,
It is I let out in the morning and barred at night.

Not a mutineer walks handcuffed to the jail, but I am
handcuffed to him and walk by his side,
I am less the jolly one there, and more the silent one with
sweat on my twitching lips.

Not a youngster is taken for larceny, but I go too and am tried
and sentenced.

Not a cholera patient lies at the last gasp, but I also lie at the
last gasp,
My face is ash-colored, my sinews gnarl .... away from me
people retreat.

Askers embody themselves in me, and I am embodied in
them,
I project my hat and sit shamefaced and beg.

I rise extatic through all, and sweep with the true gravitation,
The whirling and whirling is elemental within me.

[38]

Somehow I have been stunned. Stand back!
Give me a little time beyond my cuffed head and slumbers
and dreams and gaping,
I discover myself on a verge of the usual mistake.

That I could forget the mockers and insults!
That I could forget the trickling tears and the blows of the
bludgeons and hammers!
That I could look with a separate look on my own crucifixion
and bloody crowning!

I remember . . . . I resume the overstaid fraction,
The grave of rock multiplies what has been confided to
    it . . . . or to any graves,
The corpses rise . . . . the gashes heal . . . . the fastenings roll
    away.

I troop forth replenished with supreme power, one of an
    average unending procession,
We walk the roads of Ohio and Massachusetts and Virginia
    and Wisconsin and New York and New Orleans and
    Texas and Montreal and San Francisco and Charleston
    and Savannah and Mexico,
Inland and by the seacoast and boundary lines . . . . and we
    pass the boundary lines.

Our swift ordinances are on their way over the whole earth,
The blossoms we wear in our hats are the growth of two
    thousand years.

Eleves I salute you,
I see the approach of your numberless gangs . . . . I see you
    understand yourselves and me,
And know that they who have eyes are divine, and the blind
    and lame are equally divine,
And that my steps drag behind yours yet go before them,
And are aware how I am with you no more than I am with
    everybody.

[39]

The friendly and flowing savage . . . . Who is he?
Is he waiting for civilization or past it and mastering it?

Is he some southwesterner raised outdoors? Is he Canadian?
Is he from the Mississippi country? or from Iowa, Oregon or
    California? or from the mountain? or prairie life or
    bush-life? or from the sea?

Wherever he goes men and women accept and desire him,
They desire he should like them and touch them and speak
    to them and stay with them.

Behaviour lawless as snow-flakes . . . . words simple as
    grass . . . . uncombed head and laughter and naivete;
Slowstepping feet and the common features, and the
    common modes and emanations,
They descend in new forms from the tips of his fingers,
They are wafted with the odor of his body or breath . . . . they
    fly out of the glance of his eyes.

[40]

Flaunt of the sunshine I need not your bask . . . . lie over,
You light surfaces only . . . . I force the surfaces and the
    depths also.

Earth! you seem to look for something at my hands,
Say old topknot! what do you want?

Man or woman! I might tell how I like you, but cannot,
And might tell what it is in me and what it is in you, but cannot,
And might tell the pinings I have . . . . the pulse of my nights
    and days.

Behold I do not give lectures or a little charity,
What I give I give out of myself.

You there, impotent, loose in the knees, open your scarfed
     chops till I blow grit within you,
Spread your palms and lift the flaps of your pockets,
I am not to be denied .... I compel .... I have stores plenty
     and to spare,
And any thing I have I bestow.

I do not ask who you are .... that is not important to me,
You can do nothing and be nothing but what I will infold you.

To a drudge of the cottonfields or emptier of privies I
     lean .... on his right cheek I put the family kiss,
And in my soul I swear I never will deny him.

On women fit for conception I start bigger and nimbler babes,
This day I am jetting the stuff of far more arrogant republics.

To any one dying .... thither I speed and twist the knob of
     the door,
Turn the bedclothes toward the foot of the bed,
Let the physician and the priest go home.

I seize the descending man .... I raise him with resistless
     will.

O despairer, here is my neck,
By God! you shall not go down! Hang your whole weight
     upon me.

I dilate you with tremendous breath .... I buoy you up;
Every room of the house do I fill with an armed
     force .... lovers of me, bafflers of graves:

Sleep! I and they keep guard all night;
Not doubt, not decease shall dare to lay finger upon you,
I have embraced you, and henceforth possess you to myself,
And when you rise in the morning you will find what I tell
    you is so.

[41]

I am he bringing help for the sick as they pant on their
    backs,
And for strong upright men I bring yet more needed help.

I heard what was said of the universe,
Heard it and heard of several thousand years;
It is middling well as far as it goes . . . . but is that all?

Magnifying and applying come I,
Outbidding at the start the old cautious hucksters,
The most they offer for mankind and eternity less than a
    spirt of my own seminal wet,
Taking myself the exact dimensions of Jehovah and laying
    them away,
Lithographing Kronos and Zeus his son, and Hercules his
    grandson,
Buying drafts of Osiris and Isis and Belus and Brahma and
    Adonai,
In my portfolio placing Manito loose, and Allah on a leaf, and
    the crucifix engraved,
With Odin, and the hideous-faced Mexitli, and all idols and
    images,
Honestly taking them all for what they are worth, and not a
    cent more,
Admitting they were alive and did the work of their day,

Admitting they bore mites as for unfledged birds who have
    now to rise and fly and sing for themselves,
Accepting the rough deific sketches to fill out better in
    myself . . . . bestowing them freely on each man and
    woman I see,
Discovering as much or more in a framer framing a house,
Putting higher claims for him there with his rolled-up
    sleeves, driving the mallet and chisel;
Not objecting to special revelations . . . . considering a curl of
    smoke or a hair on the back of my hand as curious as
    any revelation;
Those ahold of fire-engines and hook-and-ladder ropes
    more to me than the gods of the antique wars,
Minding their voices peal through the crash of destruction,
Their brawny limbs passing safe over charred laths . . . . their
    white foreheads whole and unhurt out of the flames;
By the mechanic's wife with her babe at her nipple
    interceding for every person born;
Three scythes at harvest whizzing in a row from three lusty
    angels with shirts bagged out at their waists;
The snag-toothed hostler with red hair redeeming sins past
    and to come,
Selling all he possesses and traveling on foot to fee lawyers
    for his brother and sit by him while he is tried for forgery:
What was strewn in the amplest strewing the square rod
    about me, and not filling the square rod then;
The bull and the bug never worshipped half enough,
Dung and dirt more admirable than was dreamed,
The supernatural of no account . . . . myself waiting my time
    to be one of the supremes,
The day getting ready for me when I shall do as much good
    as the best, and be as prodigious,

Guessing when I am it will not tickle me much to receive
     puffs out of pulpit or print;
By my life-lumps! becoming already a creator!
Putting myself here and now to the ambushed womb of the
     shadows!

[42]

. . . . A call in the midst of the crowd,
My own voice, orotund sweeping and final.

Come my children,
Come my boys and girls, and my women and household and
     intimates,
Now the performer launches his nerve . . . . he has passed his
     prelude on the reeds within.

Easily written loosefingered chords! I feel the thrum of their
     climax and close.

My head evolves on my neck,
Music rolls, but not from the organ . . . . folks are around me,
     but they are no household of mine.

Ever the hard and unsunk ground,
Ever the eaters and drinkers . . . . ever the upward and
     downward sun . . . . ever the air and the ceaseless tides,
Ever myself and my neighbors, refreshing and wicked and
     real,
Ever the old inexplicable query . . . . ever that thorned
     thumb—that breath of itches and thirsts,
Ever the vexer's hoot! hoot! till we find where the sly one
     hides and bring him forth;

Ever love . . . . ever the sobbing liquid of life,
Ever the bandage under the chin . . . . ever the trestles of death.

Here and there with dimes on the eyes walking,
To feed the greed of the belly the brains liberally spooning,
Tickets buying or taking or selling, but in to the feast never
    once going;
Many sweating and ploughing and thrashing, and then the
    chaff for payment receiving,
A few idly owning, and they the wheat continually claiming.

This is the city . . . . and I am one of the citizens;
Whatever interests the rest interests me . . . . politics,
    churches, newspapers, schools,
Benevolent societies, improvements, banks, tariffs,
    steamships, factories, markets,
Stocks and stores and real estate and personal estate.

They who piddle and patter here in collars and tailed
    coats . . . . I am aware who they are . . . . and that they are
    not worms or fleas,
I acknowledge the duplicates of myself under all the scrape-
    lipped and pipe-legged concealments.

The weakest and shallowest is deathless with me,
What I do and say the same waits for them,
Every thought that flounders in me the same flounders in
    them.

I know perfectly well my own egotism,
And know my omnivorous words, and cannot say any less,
And would fetch you whoever you are flush with myself.

My words are words of a questioning, and to indicate reality;
This printed and bound book .... but the printer and the
    printing-office boy?
The marriage estate and settlement .... but the body and
    mind of the bridegroom? also those of the bride?
The panorama of the sea .... but the sea itself?
The well-taken photographs .... but your wife or friend
    close and solid in your arms?
The fleet of ships of the line and all the modern
    improvements .... but the craft and pluck of the
    admiral?
The dishes and fare and furniture .... but the host and
    hostess, and the look out of their eyes?
The sky up there .... yet here or next door or across the way?
The saints and sages in history .... but you yourself?
Sermons and creeds and theology .... but the human brain,
    and what is called reason, and what is called love, and
    what is called life?

[43]

I do not despise you priests;
My faith is the greatest of faiths and the least of faiths,
Enclosing all worship ancient and modern, and all between
    ancient and modern,
Believing I shall come again upon the earth after five
    thousand years,
Waiting responses from oracles .... honoring the
    gods .... saluting the sun,
Making a fetish of the first rock or stump .... powowing with
    sticks in the circle of obis,
Helping the lama or brahmin as he trims the lamps of the
    idols,

Dancing yet through the streets in a phallic
    procession . . . . rapt and austere in the woods, a
    gymnosophist,
Drinking mead from the skull-cup . . . . to shasta and vedas
    admirant . . . . minding the koran,
Walking the teokallis, spotted with gore from the stone and
    knife—beating the serpent-skin drum;
Accepting the gospels, accepting him that was crucified,
    knowing assuredly that he is divine,
To the mass kneeling—to the puritan's prayer rising—sitting
    patiently in a pew,
Ranting and frothing in my insane crisis—waiting dead-like
    till my spirit arouses me;
Looking forth on pavement and land, and outside of
    pavement and land,
Belonging to the winders of the circuit of circuits.

One of that centripetal and centrifugal gang,
I turn and talk like a man leaving charges before a
    journey.

Down-hearted doubters, dull and excluded,
Frivolous sullen moping angry affected disheartened
    atheistical,
I know every one of you, and know the unspoken
    interrogatories,
By experience I know them.

How the flukes splash!
How they contort rapid as lightning, with spasms and spouts
    of blood!

Be at peace bloody flukes of doubters and sullen mopers,
I take my place among you as much as among any;
The past is the push of you and me and all precisely the
    same,
And the day and night are for you and me and all,
And what is yet untried and afterward is for you and me
    and all.

I do not know what is untried and afterward,
But I know it is sure and alive and sufficient.

Each who passes is considered, and each who stops is
    considered, and not a single one can it fail.

It cannot fail the young man who died and was buried,
Nor the young woman who died and was put by his side,
Nor the little child that peeped in at the door and then drew
    back and was never seen again,
Nor the old man who has lived without purpose, and feels it
    with bitterness worse than gall,
Nor him in the poorhouse tubercled by rum and the bad
    disorder,
Nor the numberless slaughtered and wrecked . . . . nor the
    brutish koboo, called the ordure of humanity,
Nor the sacs merely floating with open mouths for food to
    slip in,
Nor any thing in the earth, or down in the oldest graves of
    the earth,
Nor any thing in the myriads of spheres, nor one of the
    myriads of myriads that inhabit them,
Nor the present, nor the least wisp that is known.

[44]

It is time to explain myself .... let us stand up.

What is known I strip away .... I launch all men and women
     forward with me into the unknown.

The clock indicates the moment .... but what does eternity
     indicate?
Eternity lies in bottomless reservoirs .... its buckets are
     rising forever and ever,
They pour and they pour and they exhale away.

We have thus far exhausted trillions of winters and
     summers;
There are trillions ahead, and trillions ahead of them.

Births have brought us richness and variety,
And other births will bring us richness and variety.

I do not call one greater and one smaller,
That which fills its period and place is equal to any.

Were mankind murderous or jealous upon you my brother or
     my sister?
I am sorry for you .... they are not murderous or jealous
     upon me;
All has been gentle with me .... I keep no account with
     lamentation;
What have I to do with lamentation?

I am an acme of things accomplished, and I an encloser of
     things to be.

My feet strike an apex of the apices of the stairs,
On every step bunches of ages, and larger bunches between
     the steps,
All below duly traveled—and still I mount and mount.

Rise after rise bow the phantoms behind me,
Afar down I see the huge first Nothing, the vapor from the
     nostrils of death,
I know I was even there . . . . I waited unseen and always,
And slept while God carried me through the lethargic mist,
And took my time . . . . and took no hurt from the fœtid carbon.

Long I was hugged close . . . . long and long.

Immense have been the preparations for me,
Faithful and friendly the arms that have helped me.

Cycles ferried my cradle, rowing and rowing like cheerful
     boatmen;
For room to me stars kept aside in their own rings,
They sent influences to look after what was to hold me.

Before I was born out of my mother generations guided me,
My embryo has never been torpid . . . . nothing could overlay it;
For it the nebula cohered to an orb . . . . the long slow strata
     piled to rest it on . . . . vast vegetables gave it sustenance,
Monstrous sauroids transported it in their mouths and
     deposited it with care.

All forces have been steadily employed to complete and
     delight me,
Now I stand on this spot with my soul.

[45]

Span of youth! Ever-pushed elasticity! Manhood balanced
     and florid and full!

My lovers suffocate me!
Crowding my lips, and thick in the pores of my skin,
Jostling me through streets and public halls .... coming
     naked to me at night,
Crying by day Ahoy from the rocks of the river .... swinging
     and chirping over my head,
Calling my name from flowerbeds or vines or tangled
     underbrush,
Or while I swim in the bath .... or drink from the pump at
     the corner .... or the curtain is down at the opera .... or
     I glimpse at a woman's face in the railroad car;
Lighting on every moment of my life,
Bussing my body with soft and balsamic busses,
Noiselessly passing handfuls out of their hearts and giving
     them to be mine.

Old age superbly rising! Ineffable grace of dying days!
Every condition promulges not only itself .... it promulges
     what grows after and out of itself,
And the dark hush promulges as much as any.

I open my scuttle at night and see the far-sprinkled systems,
And all I see, multiplied as high as I can cipher, edge but the
     rim of the farther systems.

Wider and wider they spread, expanding and always
     expanding,
Outward and outward and forever outward.

My sun has his sun, and round him obediently wheels,
He joins with his partners a group of superior circuit,
And greater sets follow, making specks of the greatest inside
    them.

There is no stoppage, and never can be stoppage;
If I and you and the worlds and all beneath or upon their
    surfaces, and all the palpable life, were this moment
    reduced back to a pallid float, it would not avail in the
    long run,
We should surely bring up again where we now stand,
And as surely go as much farther, and then farther and
    farther.

A few quadrillions of eras, a few octillions of cubic leagues,
    do not hazard the span, or make it impatient,
They are but parts . . . . any thing is but a part.

See ever so far . . . . there is limitless space outside of that,
Count ever so much . . . . there is limitless time around that.

Our rendezvous is fitly appointed . . . . God will be there and
    wait till we come.

[46]

I know I have the best of time and space—and that I was
    never measured, and never will be measured.

I tramp a perpetual journey,
My signs are a rain-proof coat and good shoes and a staff cut
    from the woods;
No friend of mine takes his ease in my chair,

I have no chair, nor church nor philosophy;
I lead no man to a dinner-table or library or exchange,
But each man and each woman of you I lead upon a knoll,
My left hand hooks you round the waist,
My right hand points to landscapes of continents, and a plain
     public road.

Not I, not any one else can travel that road for you,
You must travel it for yourself.

It is not far . . . . it is within reach,
Perhaps you have been on it since you were born, and did
     not know,
Perhaps it is every where on water and on land.

Shoulder your duds, and I will mine, and let us hasten
     forth;
Wonderful cities and free nations we shall fetch as we go.

If you tire, give me both burdens, and rest the chuff of your
     hand on my hip,
And in due time you shall repay the same service to me;
For after we start we never lie by again.

This day before dawn I ascended a hill and looked at the
     crowded heaven,
And I said to my spirit, When we become the enfolders of
     those orbs and the pleasure and knowledge of every
     thing in them, shall we be filled and satisfied then?
And my spirit said No, we level that lift to pass and continue
     beyond.

You are also asking me questions, and I hear you;
I answer that I cannot answer . . . . you must find out for
yourself.

Sit awhile wayfarer,
Here are biscuits to eat and here is milk to drink,
But as soon as you sleep and renew yourself in sweet clothes
I will certainly kiss you with my goodbye kiss and open
the gate for your egress hence.

Long enough have you dreamed contemptible dreams,
Now I wash the gum from your eyes,
You must habit yourself to the dazzle of the light and of
every moment of your life.

Long have you timidly waded, holding a plank by the shore,
Now I will you to be a bold swimmer,
To jump off in the midst of the sea, and rise again and nod to
me and shout, and laughingly dash with your hair.

[47]

I am the teacher of athletes,
He that by me spreads a wider breast than my own proves
the width of my own,
He most honors my style who learns under it to destroy the
teacher.

The boy I love, the same becomes a man not through derived
power but in his own right,
Wicked, rather than virtuous out of conformity or fear,
Fond of his sweetheart, relishing well his steak,

Unrequited love or a slight cutting him worse than a wound
    cuts,
First rate to ride, to fight, to hit the bull's eye, to sail a skiff, to
    sing a song or play on the banjo,
Preferring scars and faces pitted with smallpox over all
    latherers and those that keep out of the sun.

I teach straying from me, yet who can stray from me?
I follow you whoever you are from the present hour;
My words itch at your ears till you understand them.

I do not say these things for a dollar, or to fill up the time
    while I wait for a boat;
It is you talking just as much as myself . . . . I act as the
    tongue of you,
It was tied in your mouth . . . . in mine it begins to be loosened.

I swear I will never mention love or death inside a house,
And I swear I never will translate myself at all, only to him or
    her who privately stays with me in the open air.

If you would understand me go to the heights or water-shore,
The nearest gnat is an explanation and a drop or the motion
    of waves a key,
The maul the oar and the handsaw second my words.

No shuttered room or school can commune with me,
But roughs and little children better than they.

The young mechanic is closest to me . . . . he knows me pretty
    well,

The woodman that takes his axe and jug with him shall take
    me with him all day,
The farmboy ploughing in the field feels good at the sound of
    my voice,
In vessels that sail my words must sail . . . . I go with
    fishermen and seamen, and love them,
My face rubs to the hunter's face when he lies down alone in
    his blanket,
The driver thinking of me does not mind the jolt of his
    wagon,
The young mother and old mother shall comprehend me,
The girl and the wife rest the needle a moment and forget
    where they are,
They and all would resume what I have told them.

[48]

I have said that the soul is not more than the body,
And I have said that the body is not more than the soul,
And nothing, not God, is greater to one than one's-self is,
And whoever walks a furlong without sympathy walks to his
    own funeral, dressed in his shroud,
And I or you pocketless of a dime may purchase the pick of
    the earth,
And to glance with an eye or show a bean in its pod
    confounds the learning of all times,
And there is no trade or employment but the young man
    following it may become a hero,
And there is no object so soft but it makes a hub for the
    wheeled universe,
And any man or woman shall stand cool and supercilious
    before a million universes.

And I call to mankind, Be not curious about God,
For I who am curious about each am not curious about God,
No array of terms can say how much I am at peace about
    God and about death.

I hear and behold God in every object, yet I understand God
    not in the least,
Nor do I understand who there can be more wonderful than
    myself.

Why should I wish to see God better than this day?
I see something of God each hour of the twenty-four, and
    each moment then,
In the faces of men and women I see God, and in my own
    face in the glass;
I find letters from God dropped in the street, and every one
    is signed by God's name,
And I leave them where they are, for I know that others will
    punctually come forever and ever.

[49]

And as to you death, and you bitter hug of mortality . . . . it is
    idle to try to alarm me.

To his work without flinching the accoucheur comes,
I see the elderhand pressing receiving supporting,
I recline by the sills of the exquisite flexible doors . . . . and
    mark the outlet, and mark the relief and escape.

And as to you corpse I think you are good manure, but that
    does not offend me,
I smell the white roses sweetscented and growing,

I reach to the leafy lips .... I reach to the polished breasts of
    melons,

And as to you life, I reckon you are the leavings of many deaths,
No doubt I have died myself ten thousand times before.

I hear you whispering there O stars of heaven,
O suns .... O grass of graves .... O perpetual transfers and
    promotions .... if you do not say anything how can I say
    anything?

Of the turbid pool that lies in the autumn forest,
Of the moon that descends the steeps of the soughing
    twilight,
Toss, sparkles of day and dusk .... toss on the black stems
    that decay in the muck,
Toss to the moaning gibberish of the dry limbs.

I ascend from the moon .... I ascend from the night,
And perceive of the ghastly glitter the sunbeams reflected,
And debouch to the steady and central from the offspring
    great or small.

[50]

There is that in me .... I do not know what it is .... but I
    know it is in me.
Wrenched and sweaty .... calm and cool then my body
    becomes;
I sleep .... I sleep long.

I do not know it .... it is without name .... it is a word unsaid,
It is not in any dictionary or utterance or symbol.

Something it swings on more than the earth I swing on,
To it the creation is the friend whose embracing awakes me.

Perhaps I might tell more . . . . Outlines! I plead for my
      brothers and sisters.

Do you see O my brothers and sisters?
It is not chaos or death . . . . it is form and union and
      plan . . . . it is eternal life . . . . it is happiness.

[51]

The past and present wilt . . . . I have filled them and emptied
      them,
And proceed to fill my next fold of the future.

Listener up there! Here you . . . . what have you to confide to
      me?
Look in my face while I snuff the sidle of evening,
Talk honestly, for no one else hears you, and I stay only a
      minute longer.

Do I contradict myself?
Very well then . . . . I contradict myself;
I am large . . . . I contain multitudes.

I concentrate toward them that are nigh . . . . I wait on the
      door-slab.

Who has done his day's work and will soonest be through
      with his supper?
Who wishes to walk with me?

Will you speak before I am gone? Will you prove already too
    late?

[52]

The spotted hawk swoops by and accuses me . . . . he
    complains of my gab and my loitering.

I too am not a bit tamed . . . . I too am untranslatable,
I sound my barbaric yawp over the roofs of the world.

The last scud of day holds back for me,
It flings my likeness after the rest and true as any on the
    shadowed wilds,
It coaxes me to the vapor and the dusk.

I depart as air . . . . I shake my white locks at the runaway sun,
I effuse my flesh in eddies and drift it in lacy jags.

I bequeath myself to the dirt to grow from the grass I love,
If you want me again look for me under your bootsoles.

You will hardly know who I am or what I mean,
But I shall be good health to you nevertheless,
And filter and fibre your blood.

Failing to fetch me at first keep encouraged,
Missing me one place search another,
I stop some where waiting for you

LEAVES OF GRASS

[A Song for Occupations]

[1]

Come closer to me,
Push close my lovers and take the best I possess,
Yield closer and closer and give me the best you possess.

This is unfinished business with me .... how is it with you?
I was chilled with the cold types and cylinder and wet paper
    between us.

I pass so poorly with paper and types .... I must pass with
    the contact of bodies and souls.

I do not thank you for liking me as I am, and liking the touch
    of me .... I know that it is good for you to do so.

Were all educations practical and ornamental well displayed
    out of me, what would it amount to?
Were I as the head teacher or charitable proprietor or wise
    statesman, what would it amount to?
Were I to you as the boss employing and paying you, would
    that satisfy you?

The learned and virtuous and benevolent, and the usual terms;
A man like me, and never the usual terms.

Neither a servant nor a master am I,
I take no sooner a large price than a small price .... I will
    have my own whoever enjoys me,
I will be even with you, and you shall be even with me.

If you are a workman or workwoman I stand as nigh as the
    nighest that works in the same shop,
If you bestow gifts on your brother or dearest friend, I
    demand as good as your brother or dearest friend,
If your lover or husband or wife is welcome by day or night, I
    must be personally as welcome;
If you have become degraded or ill, then I will become so for
    your sake;
If you remember your foolish and outlawed deeds, do you
    think I cannot remember my foolish and outlawed
    deeds?
If you carouse at the table I say I will carouse at the opposite
    side of the table;
If you meet some stranger in the street and love him or her,
    do I not often meet strangers in the street and love
    them?
If you see a good deal remarkable in me I see just as much
    remarkable in you.

Why what have you thought of yourself?
Is it you then that thought yourself less?
Is it you that thought the President greater than you? or the
    rich better off than you? or the educated wiser than you?

Because you are greasy or pimpled—or that you was once
    drunk, or a thief, or diseased, or rheumatic, or a

prostitute—or are so now—or from frivolity or
impotence—or that you are no scholar, and never saw
your name in print . . . . do you give in that you are any
less immortal?

[2]

Souls of men and women! it is not you I call unseen,
    unheard, untouchable and untouching;
It is not you I go argue pro and con about, and to settle
    whether you are alive or no;
I own publicly who you are, if nobody else owns . . . . and see
    and hear you, and what you give and take;
What is there you cannot give and take?

I see not merely that you are polite or
    whitefaced . . . . married or single . . . . citizens of old
    states or citizens of new states . . . . eminent in some
    profession . . . . a lady or gentleman in a parlor . . . . or
    dressed in the jail uniform . . . . or pulpit uniform,
Not only the free Utahan, Kansian, or Arkansian . . . . not only
    the free Cuban . . . not merely the slave . . . . not Mexican
    native, or Flatfoot, or negro from Africa,
Iroquois eating the warflesh—fishtearer in his lair of rocks
    and sand . . . . Esquimaux in the dark cold
    snowhouse . . . . Chinese with his transverse
    eyes. . . . Bedowee—or wandering nomad—or
    tabounschik at the head of his droves,
Grown, half-grown, and babe—of this country and every
    country, indoors and outdoors I see . . . . and all else is
    behind or through them.

The wife—and she is not one jot less than the husband,
The daughter—and she is just as good as the son,
The mother—and she is every bit as much as the
     father.

Offspring of those not rich—boys apprenticed to trades,
Young fellows working on farms and old fellows working on
     farms;
The naive . . . . the simple and hardy . . . . he going to the polls
     to vote . . . . he who has a good time, and he who has a
     bad time;
Mechanics, southerners, new arrivals, sailors, mano'warsmen,
     merchantmen, coasters,
All these I see . . . . but nigher and farther the same I see;
None shall escape me, and none shall wish to escape me.

I bring what you much need, yet always have,
I bring not money or amours or dress or eating . . . . but I
     bring as good;
And send no agent or medium . . . . and offer no
     representative of value—but offer the value itself.

There is something that comes home to one now and
     perpetually,
It is not what is printed or preached or discussed . . . . it
     eludes discussion and print,
It is not to be put in a book . . . . it is not in this book,
It is for you whoever you are . . . . it is no farther from you
     than your hearing and sight are from you,
It is hinted by nearest and commonest and readiest . . . . it is
     not them, though it is endlessly provoked by
     them . . . . What is there ready and near you now?

You may read in many languages and read nothing about it;
You may read the President's message and read nothing
about it there;
Nothing in the reports from the state department or treasury
department . . . . or in the daily papers, or the weekly
papers,
Or in the census returns or assessors' returns or prices
current or any accounts of stock.

[3]

The sun and stars that float in the open air . . . . the
appleshaped earth and we upon it . . . . surely the drift of
them is something grand;
I do not know what it is except that it is grand, and that it is
happiness,
And that the enclosing purport of us here is not a
speculation, or bon-mot or reconnoissance,
And that it is not something which by luck may turn out well
for us, and without luck must be a failure for us,
And not something which may yet be retracted in a certain
contingency.

The light and shade—the curious sense of body and
identity—the greed that with perfect complaisance
devours all things—the endless pride and outstretching
of man—unspeakable joys and sorrows,
The wonder every one sees in every one else he sees . . . . and
the wonders that fill each minute of time forever and
each acre of surface and space forever,
Have you reckoned them as mainly for a trade or farmwork? or
for the profits of a store? or to achieve yourself a position?
or to fill a gentleman's leisure or a lady's leisure?

Have you reckoned the landscape took substance and form
    that it might be painted in a picture?
Or men and women that they might be written of, and songs
    sung?
Or the attraction of gravity and the great laws and
    harmonious combinations and the fluids of the air as
    subjects for the savans?
Or the brown land and the blue sea for maps and charts?
Or the stars to be put in constellations and named fancy
    names?
Or that the growth of seeds is for agricultural tables or
    agriculture itself?

Old institutions . . . . these arts libraries legends collections—
    and the practice handed along in manufactures . . . . will
    we rate them so high?
Will we rate our prudence and business so high? . . . . I have
    no objection,
I rate them as high as the highest . . . . but a child born of a
    woman and man I rate beyond all rate.

We thought our Union grand and our Constitution grand;
I do not say they are not grand and good—for they are,
I am this day just as much in love with them as you,
But I am eternally in love with you and with all my fellows
    upon the earth.

We consider the bibles and religions divine . . . . I do not say
    they are not divine,
I say they have all grown out of you and may grow out of you
    still,
It is not they who give the life . . . . it is you who give the life;

Leaves are not more shed from the trees or trees from the
earth than they are shed out of you.

[4]

The sum of all known value and respect I add up in you
whoever you are;
The President is up there in the White House for you . . . . it
is not you who are here for him,
The Secretaries act in their bureaus for you . . . . not you here
for them,
The Congress convenes every December for you,
Laws, courts, the forming of states, the charters of cities, the
going and coming of commerce and mails are all for you.

All doctrines, all politics and civilization exurge from you,
All sculpture and monuments and anything inscribed
anywhere are tallied in you,
The gist of histories and statistics as far back as the records
reach is in you this hour—and myths and tales the same;
If you were not breathing and walking here where would
they all be?
The most renowned poems would be ashes . . . . orations and
plays would be vacuums.

All architecture is what you do to it when you look upon it;
Did you think it was in the white or gray stone? or the lines
of the arches and cornices?

All music is what awakens from you when you are reminded
by the instruments,
It is not the violins and the cornets . . . . it is not the oboe nor
the beating drums—nor the notes of the baritone singer

singing his sweet romanza . . . . nor those of the men's
    chorus, nor those of the women's chorus,
It is nearer and farther than they.

[5]

Will the whole come back then?
Can each see the signs of the best by a look in the
    lookingglass? Is there nothing greater or more?
Does all sit there with you and here with me?

The old forever new things . . . . you foolish child! . . . . the
    closest simplest things—this moment with you,
Your person and every particle that relates to your person,
The pulses of your brain waiting their chance and
    encouragement at every deed or sight;
Anything you do in public by day, and anything you do in
    secret betweendays,
What is called right and what is called wrong . . . . what you
    behold or touch . . . . what causes your anger or wonder,
The anklechain of the slave, the bed of the bedhouse, the
    cards of the gambler, the plates of the forger;
What is seen or learned in the street, or intuitively learned,
What is learned in the public school—spelling, reading,
    writing and ciphering . . . . the blackboard and the
    teacher's diagrams:
The panes of the windows and all that appears through
    them . . . . the going forth in the morning and the aimless
    spending of the day;
(What is it that you made money? what is it that you got
    what you wanted?)
The usual routine . . . . the workshop, factory, yard, office,
    store, or desk;

The jaunt of hunting or fishing, or the life of hunting or fishing,
Pasturelife, foddering, milking and herding, and all the
      personnel and usages;
The plum-orchard and apple-orchard .... gardening ....
      seedlings, cuttings, flowers and vines,
Grains and manures .. marl, clay, loam .. the subsoil
      plough .. the shovel and pick and rake and
      hoe .. irrigation and draining;
The currycomb .. the horse-cloth .. the halter and bridle and
      bits .. the very wisps of straw,
The barn and barn-yard .. the bins and mangers .. the mows
      and racks:
Manufactures .. commerce .. engineering .. the building of
      cities, and every trade carried on there .. and the
      implements of every trade,
The anvil and tongs and hammer .. the axe and wedge .. the
      square and mitre and jointer and smoothingplane;
The plumbob and trowel and level .. the wall-scaffold, and
      the work of walls and ceilings .. or any mason-work:
The ship's compass .. the sailor's tarpaulin .. the stays and
      lanyards, and the ground-tackle for anchoring or mooring,
The sloop's tiller .. the pilot's wheel and bell .. the yacht or
      fish-smack .. the great gay-pennanted three-hundred-
      foot steamboat under full headway, with her proud fat
      breasts and her delicate swift-flashing paddles;
The trail and line and hooks and sinkers .. the seine, and
      hauling the seine;
Smallarms and rifles .... the powder and shot and caps and
      wadding .... the ordnance for war .... the carriages:
Everyday objects .... the housechairs, the carpet, the bed
      and the counterpane of the bed, and him or her sleeping
      at night, and the wind blowing, and the indefinite noises:

The snowstorm or rainstorm . . . . the tow-trowsers . . . . the
    lodge-hut in the woods, and the still-hunt:

City and country . . fireplace and candle . . gaslight and
    heater and aqueduct;

The message of the governor, mayor, or chief of
    police . . . . the dishes of breakfast or dinner or supper;

The bunkroom, the fire-engine, the string-team, and the car
    or truck behind;

The paper I write on or you write on . . and every word we
    write . . and every cross and twirl of the pen . . and the
    curious way we write what we think . . . . yet very
    faintly;

The directory, the detector, the ledger . . . . the books in ranks
    or the bookshelves. . . . the clock attached to the wall,

The ring on your finger . . the lady's wristlet . . the hammers
    of stonebreakers or coppersmiths . . the druggist's vials
    and jars;

The etui of surgical instruments, and the etui of oculist's or
    aurist's instruments, or dentist's instruments;

Glassblowing, grinding of wheat and corn . . casting, and
    what is cast . . tinroofing, shingledressing,

Shipcarpentering, flagging of sidewalks by
    flaggers . . dockbuilding, fishcuring, ferrying;

The pump, the piledriver, the great derrick . . the coalkiln and
    brickkiln,

Ironworks or whiteleadworks . . the sugarhouse . . steam-
    saws, and the great mills and factories;

The cottonbale . . the stevedore's hook . . the saw and buck of
    the sawyer . . the screen of the coalscreener . . the mould
    of the moulder . . the workingknife of the butcher;

The cylinder press . . the handpress . . the frisket and
    tympan . . the compositor's stick and rule,

The implements for daguerreotyping . . . . the tools of the
    rigger or grappler or sailmaker or blockmaker,
Goods of guttapercha or papiermache . . . . colors and
    brushes . . . . glaziers' implements,
The veneer and gluepot . . the confectioner's ornaments . .
    the decanter and glasses . . the shears and flatiron;
The awl and kneestrap . . the pint measure and quart
    measure . . the counter and stool . . the writingpen of
    quill or metal;
Billiards and tenpins . . . . the ladders and hanging ropes of
    the gymnasium, and the manly exercises;
The designs for wallpapers or oilcloths or carpets . . . . the
    fancies for goods for women . . . . the bookbinder's stamps;
Leatherdressing, coachmaking, boilermaking, ropetwisting,
    distilling, signpainting, limeburning, coopering,
    cottonpicking,
The walkingbeam of the steam-engine . . the throttle and
    governors, and the up and down rods,
Stavemachines and planingmachines . . . . the cart of the
    carman . . the omnibus . . the ponderous dray;
The snowplough and two engines pushing it . . . . the ride
    in the express train of only one car . . . . the swift go
    through a howling storm:
The bearhunt or coonhunt . . . . the bonfire of shavings in the
    open lot in the city . . the crowd of children watching;
The blows of the fighting-man . . the upper cut and one-two-
    three;
The shopwindows . . . . the coffins in the sexton's
    wareroom . . . . the fruit on the fruitstand . . . . the beef
    on the butcher's stall,
The bread and cakes in the bakery . . . . the white and red
    pork in the pork-store;

The milliner's ribbons . . the dressmaker's patterns . . . . the
      tea-table . . the homemade sweetmeats:
The column of wants in the one-cent paper . . the news by
      telegraph . . . . the amusements and operas and shows:
The cotton and woolen and linen you wear . . . . the money
      you make and spend;
Your room and bedroom . . . . your piano-forte . . . . the stove
      and cookpans,
The house you live in . . . . the rent . . . . the other
      tenants . . . . the deposit in the savings-bank . . . . the
      trade at the grocery,
The pay on Saturday night . . . . the going home, and the
      purchases;
In them the heft of the heaviest . . . . in them far more than
      you estimated, and far less also,
In them, not yourself . . . . you and your soul enclose all
      things, regardless of estimation,
In them your themes and hints and provokers . . if not, the
      whole earth has no themes or hints or provokers, and
      never had.

I do not affirm what you see beyond is futile . . . . I do not
      advise you to stop,
I do not say leadings you thought great are not great,
But I say that none lead to greater or sadder or happier than
      those lead to.

[6]

Will you seek afar off? You surely come back at last,
In things best known to you finding the best or as good as
      the best,

In folks nearest to you finding also the sweetest and
    strongest and lovingest,
Happiness not in another place, but this place .. not for
    another hour, but this hour,
Man in the first you see or touch .... always in your friend or
    brother or nighest neighbor .... Woman in your mother
    or lover or wife,
And all else thus far known giving place to men and women.

When the psalm sings instead of the singer,
When the script preaches instead of the preacher,
When the pulpit descends and goes instead of the carver that
    carved the supporting desk,
When the sacred vessels or the bits of the eucharist, or the
    lath and plast, procreate as effectually as the young
    silversmiths or bakers, or the masons in their overalls,
When a university course convinces like a slumbering
    woman and child convince,
When the minted gold in the vault smiles like the
    nightwatchman's daughter,
When warrantee deeds loafe in chairs opposite and are my
    friendly companions,
I intend to reach them my hand and make as much of them
    as I do of men and women.

LEAVES OF GRASS

[To Think of Time]

[1]

To think of time .... to think through the retrospection,
To think of today .. and the ages continued henceforward.
Have you guessed you yourself would not continue? Have
    you dreaded those earth-beetles?
Have you feared the future would be nothing to you?

Is today nothing? Is the beginningless past nothing?
If the future is nothing they are just as surely nothing.

To think that the sun rose in the east .... that men and
    women were flexible and real and alive .... that every
    thing was real and alive;
To think that you and I did not see feel think nor bear our
    part,
To think that we are now here and bear our part.

[2]

Not a day passes .. not a minute or second without an
    accouchement;
Not a day passes .. not a minute or second without a corpse.

When the dull nights are over, and the dull days also,
When the soreness of lying so much in bed is over,
When the physician, after long putting off, gives the silent
     and terrible look for an answer,
When the children come hurried and weeping, and the
     brothers and sisters have been sent for,
When medicines stand unused on the shelf, and the
     camphor-smell has pervaded the rooms,
When the faithful hand of the living does not desert the
     hand of the dying,
When the twitching lips press lightly on the forehead of the
     dying,
When the breath ceases and the pulse of the heart ceases,
Then the corpse-limbs stretch on the bed, and the living look
     upon them,
They are palpable as the living are palpable.

The living look upon the corpse with their eyesight,
But without eyesight lingers a different living and looks
     curiously on the corpse.

[3]

To think that the rivers will come to flow, and the snow fall,
     and fruits ripen . . and act upon others as upon us
     now . . . . yet not act upon us;
To think of all these wonders of city and country . . and
     others taking great interest in them . . and we taking
     small interest in them.

To think how eager we are in building our houses,
To think others shall be just as eager . . and we quite
     indifferent.

I see one building the house that serves him a few
    years . . . . or seventy or eighty years at most;
I see one building the house that serves him longer than that.

Slowmoving and black lines creep over the whole
    earth . . . . they never cease . . . . they are the burial lines,
He that was President was buried, and he that is now
    President shall surely be buried.

[4]

Cold dash of waves at the ferrywharf,
Posh and ice in the river . . . . half-frozen mud in the streets,
A gray discouraged sky overhead . . . . the short last daylight
    of December,
A hearse and stages . . . . other vehicles give place,
The funeral of an old stagedriver . . . . the cortege mostly drivers.

Rapid the trot to the cemetery,
Duly rattles the deathbell . . . . the gate is passed . . . . the
    grave is halted at . . . . the living alight . . . . the hearse
    uncloses,
The coffin is lowered and settled . . . . the whip is laid on the
    coffin,
The earth is swiftly shovelled in . . . . a minute . . no one
    moves or speaks . . . . it is done,
He is decently put away . . . . is there anything more?

He was a goodfellow,
Freemouthed, quicktempered, not badlooking, able to take
    his own part,
Witty, sensitive to a slight, ready with life or death for a
    friend,

Fond of women, . . played some . . eat hearty and drank hearty,
Had known what it was to be flush . . grew lowspirited toward
    the last . . sickened . . was helped by a contribution,
Died aged forty-one years . . and that was his funeral.

Thumb extended or finger uplifted,
Apron, cape, gloves, strap . . . . wetweather clothes . . . . whip
    carefully chosen . . . . boss, spotter, starter, and hostler,
Somebody loafing on you, or you loafing on somebody . . . .
    headway . . . . man before and man behind,
Good day's work or bad day's work . . . . pet stock or mean
    stock . . . . first out or last out . . . . turning in at night,
To think that these are so much and so nigh to other
    drivers . . . . and he there takes no interest in them.

[5]

The markets, the government, the workingman's wages . . . . to
    think what account they are through our nights and days;
To think that other workingmen will make just as great
    account of them . . yet we make little or no account.

The vulgar and the refined . . . . what you call sin and what
    you call goodness . . to think how wide a difference;
To think the difference will still continue to others, yet we lie
    beyond the difference.

To think how much pleasure there is!
Have you pleasure from looking at the sky? Have you
    pleasure from poems?
Do you enjoy yourself in the city? or engaged in business? or
    planning a nomination and election? or with your wife
    and family?

Or with your mother and sisters? or in womanly housework?
    or the beautiful maternal cares?

These also flow onward to others . . . . you and I flow
    onward;
But in due time you and I shall take less interest in them.

Your farm and profits and crops . . . . to think how engrossed
    you are;
To think there will still be farms and profits and crops . . yet
    for you of what avail?

[6]

What will be will be well—for what is is well,
To take interest is well, and not to take interest shall
    be well.

The sky continues beautiful . . . . the pleasure of men with
    women shall never be sated . . nor the pleasure of
    women with men . . nor the pleasure from poems;
The domestic joys, the daily housework or business, the
    building of houses—they are not phantasms . . they have
    weight and form and location;
The farms and profits and crops . . the markets and wages
    and government . . they also are not phantasms;
The difference between sin and goodness is no apparition;
The earth is not an echo . . . . man and his life and all the
    things of his life are well-considered.

You are not thrown to the winds . . you gather certainly and
    safely around yourself,
Yourself! Yourself! Yourself forever and ever!

[7]

It is not to diffuse you that you were born of your mother and
    father—it is to identify you,
It is not that you should be undecided, but that you should be
    decided;
Something long preparing and formless is arrived and
    formed in you,
You are thenceforth secure, whatever comes or goes.

The threads that were spun are gathered . . . . the weft
    crosses the warp . . . . the pattern is systematic.

The preparations have every one been justified;
The orchestra have tuned their instruments
    sufficiently . . . . the baton has given the signal.

The guest that was coming . . . . he waited long for
    reasons . . . . he is now housed,
He is one of those who are beautiful and happy . . . . he is one
    of those that to look upon and be with is enough.

The law of the past cannot be eluded,
The law of the present and future cannot be eluded,
The law of the living cannot be eluded . . . . it is eternal,
The law of promotion and transformation cannot be eluded,
The law of heroes and good-doers cannot be eluded,
The law of drunkards and informers and mean persons
    cannot be eluded.

[8]

Slowmoving and black lines go ceaselessly over the earth,
Northerner goes carried and southerner goes carried . . . .

and they on the Atlantic side and they on the Pacific, and
   they between, and all through the Mississippi
   country . . . . and all over the earth.
The great masters and kosmos are well as they go . . . . the
   heroes and good-doers are well,
The known leaders and inventors and the rich owners and
   pious and distinguished may be well,
But there is more account than that . . . . there is strict
   account of all.

The interminable hordes of the ignorant and wicked are not
   nothing,
The barbarians of Africa and Asia are not nothing,
The common people of Europe are not nothing . . . . the
   American aborigines are not nothing,
A zambo or a foreheadless Crowfoot or a Camanche is not
   nothing,
The infected in the immigrant hospital are not
   nothing . . . . the murderer or mean person is not
   nothing,
The perpetual succession of shallow people are not nothing
   as they go,
The prostitute is not nothing . . . . the mocker of religion is
   not nothing as he goes.

I shall go with the rest . . . . we have satisfaction:
I have dreamed that we are not to be changed so
   much . . . . nor the law of us changed;
I have dreamed that heroes and good-doers shall be under
   the present and past law,
And that murderers and drunkards and liars shall be under
   the present and past law;

For I have dreamed that the law they are under now is
    enough.

And I have dreamed that the satisfaction is not so much
    changed . . . . and that there is no life without
    satisfaction;
What is the earth? what are body and soul without satisfaction?

I shall go with the rest,
We cannot be stopped at a given point . . . . that is no
    satisfaction;
To show us a good thing or a few good things for a space of
    time—that is no satisfaction;
We must have the indestructible breed of the best, regardless
    of time.

If otherwise, all these things came but to ashes of dung;
If maggots and rats ended us, then suspicion and treachery
    and death.

Do you suspect death? If I were to suspect death I should die
    now,
Do you think I could walk pleasantly and well-suited toward
    annihilation?

Pleasantly and well-suited I walk,
Whither I walk I cannot define, but I know it is good,
The whole universe indicates that it is good,
The past and the present indicate that it is good.

How beautiful and perfect are the animals! How perfect is
    my soul!

How perfect the earth, and the minutest thing upon it!
What is called good is perfect, and what is called sin is just as
    perfect;
The vegetables and minerals are all perfect . . and the
    imponderable fluids are perfect;
Slowly and surely they have passed on to this, and slowly
    and surely they will yet pass on.

O my soul! if I realize you I have satisfaction,
Animals and vegetables! if I realize you I have satisfaction,
Laws of the earth and air! if I realize you I have satisfaction.

I cannot define my satisfaction . . yet it is so,
I cannot define my life . . yet it is so.

[9]

I swear I see now that every thing has an eternal soul!
The trees have, rooted in the ground . . . . the weeds of the
    sea have . . . . the animals.

I swear I think there is nothing but immortality!
That the exquisite scheme is for it, and the nebulous float is
    for it, and the cohering is for it,
And all preparation is for it . . and identity is for it . . and life
    and death are for it.

LEAVES OF GRASS

[The Sleepers]

[1]

I wander all night in my vision,

Stepping with light feet .... swiftly and noiselessly stepping
and stopping,

Bending with open eyes over the shut eyes of sleepers;

Wandering and confused .... lost to myself .... ill-
assorted .... contradictory,

Pausing and gazing and bending and stopping.

How solemn they look there, stretched and still;

How quiet they breathe, the little children in their cradles.

The wretched features of ennuyees, the white features of
corpses, the livid faces of drunkards, the sick-gray faces
of onanists,

The gashed bodies on battlefields, the insane in their strong-
doored rooms, the sacred idiots,

The newborn emerging from gates and the dying emerging
from gates,

The night pervades them and enfolds them.

The married couple sleep calmly in their bed, he with his
palm on the hip of the wife, and she with her palm on
the hip of the husband,

The sisters sleep lovingly side by side in their bed,
The men sleep lovingly side by side in theirs,
And the mother sleeps with her little child carefully wrapped.
The blind sleep, and the deaf and dumb sleep,
The prisoner sleeps well in the prison . . . . the runaway son
     sleeps,
The murderer that is to be hung next day . . . . how does he
     sleep?
And the murdered person . . . . how does he sleep?

The female that loves unrequited sleeps,
And the male that loves unrequited sleeps;
The head of the moneymaker that plotted all day sleeps,
And the enraged and treacherous dispositions sleep.

I stand with drooping eyes by the worstsuffering and
     restless,
I pass my hands soothingly to and fro a few inches from
     them;
The restless sink in their beds . . . . they fitfully sleep.

The earth recedes from me into the night,
I saw that it was beautiful . . . . and I see that what is not the
     earth is beautiful.

I go from bedside to bedside . . . . I sleep close with the other
     sleepers, each in turn;
I dream in my dream all the dreams of the other dreamers,
And I become the other dreamers.

I am a dance . . . . Play up there! the fit is whirling me fast.

I am the everlaughing . . . . it is new moon and twilight,
I see the hiding of douceurs . . . . I see nimble ghosts
    whichever way I look,
Cache and cache again deep in the ground and sea, and
    where it is neither ground or sea.

Well do they do their jobs, those journeymen divine,
Only from me can they hide nothing and would not if they
    could;
I reckon I am their boss, and they make me a pet besides,
And surround me, and lead me and run ahead when I walk,
And lift their cunning covers and signify me with stretched
    arms, and resume the way;
Onward we move, a gay gang of blackguards with
    mirthshouting music and wildflapping pennants of joy.

I am the actor and the actress . . . . the voter . . the politician,
The emigrant and the exile . . the criminal that stood in the
    box,
He who has been famous, and he who shall be famous after
    today,
The stammerer . . . . the wellformed person . . the wasted or
    feeble person.

I am she who adorned herself and folded her hair
    expectantly,
My truant lover has come and it is dark.

Double yourself and receive me darkness,
Receive me and my lover too . . . . he will not let me go
    without him.

I roll myself upon you as upon a bed . . . . I resign myself to
    the dusk.

He whom I call answers me and takes the place of my lover,
He rises with me silently from the bed.

Darkness you are gentler than my lover . . . . his flesh was
    sweaty and panting,
I feel the hot moisture yet that he left me.

My hands are spread forth . . I pass them in all directions,
I would sound up the shadowy shore to which you are
    journeying.

Be careful, darkness . . . . already, what was it touched me?
I thought my lover had gone . . . . else darkness and he are
    one,
I hear the heart-beat . . . . I follow . . I fade away.

O hotcheeked and blushing! O foolish hectic!
O for pity's sake, no one must see me now! . . . . my clothes
    were stolen while I was abed,
Now I am thrust forth, where shall I run?

Pier that I saw dimly last night when I looked from the
    windows,
Pier out from the main, let me catch myself with you and
    stay . . . . I will not chafe you;
I feel ashamed to go naked about the world,
And am curious to know where my feet stand . . . . and what
    is this flooding me, childhood or manhood . . . . and the
    hunger that crosses the bridge between.

The cloth laps a first sweet eating and drinking,
Laps life-swelling yolks .... laps ear of rose-corn, milky and
    just ripened:
The white teeth stay, and the boss-tooth advances in darkness,
And liquor is spilled on lips and bosoms by touching glasses,
    and the best liquor afterward.

[2]

I descend my western course .... my sinews are flaccid,
Perfume and youth course through me, and I am their wake.

It is my face yellow and wrinkled instead of the old woman's,
I sit low in a strawbottom chair and carefully darn my
    grandson's stockings.

It is I too .... the sleepless widow looking out on the winter
    midnight,
I see the sparkles of starshine on the icy and pallid earth.

A shroud I see—and I am the shroud .... I wrap a body and
    lie in the coffin;
It is dark here underground .... it is not evil or pain
    here .... it is blank here, for reasons.

It seems to me that everything in the light and air ought to
    be happy;
Whoever is not in his coffin and the dark grave, let him know
    he has enough.

[3]

I see a beautiful gigantic swimmer swimming naked through
    the eddies of the sea,

His brown hair lies close and even to his head . . . . he strikes
    out with courageous arms . . . . he urges himself with his
    legs.

I see his white body . . . . I see his undaunted eyes;
I hate the swift-running eddies that would dash him
    headforemost on the rocks.

What are you doing you ruffianly red-trickled waves?
Will you kill the courageous giant? Will you kill him in the
    prime of his middle age?

Steady and long he struggles;
He is baffled and banged and bruised . . . . he holds out while
    his strength holds out,
The slapping eddies are spotted with his blood . . . . they
    bear him away . . . . they roll him and swing him and
    turn him:
His beautiful body is borne in the circling eddies . . . . it is
    continually bruised on rocks,
Swiftly and out of sight is borne the brave corpse.

[4]

I turn but do not extricate myself;
Confused . . . . a pastreading . . . . another, but with darkness
    yet.

The beach is cut by the razory ice-wind . . . . the wreck-guns
    sounds,
The tempest lulls and the moon comes floundering through
    the drifts.

I look where the ship helplessly heads end on . . . . I hear the
    burst as she strikes . . I hear the howls of dismay . . . . they
    grow fainter and fainter.

I cannot aid with my wringing fingers;
I can but rush to the surf and let it drench me and freeze
    upon me.

I search with the crowd . . . . not one of the company is
    washed to us alive;
In the morning I help pick up the dead and lay them in rows
    in a barn.

[5]

Now of the old war-days . . the defeat at Brooklyn;
Washington stands inside the lines . . he stands on the
    entrenched hills amid a crowd of officers,
His face is cold and damp . . . . he cannot repress the weeping
    drops . . . . he lifts the glass perpetually to his
    eyes . . . . the color is blanched from his cheeks,
He sees the slaughter of the southern braves confided to him
    by their parents.

The same at last and at last when peace is declared,
He stands in the room of the old tavern . . . . the wellbeloved
    soldiers all pass through.

The officers speechless and slow draw near in their
    turns,
The chief encircles their necks with his arm and kisses them
    on the cheek,

He kisses lightly the wet cheeks one after another . . . . he
    shakes hands and bids goodbye to the army.

[6]

Now I tell what my mother told me today as we sat at dinner
    together,
Of when she was a nearly grown girl living home with her
    parents on the old homestead.

A red squaw came one breakfasttime to the old homestead,
On her back she carried a bundle of rushes for
    rushbottoming chairs;
Her hair straight shiny coarse black and profuse
    halfenveloped her face,
Her step was free and elastic . . . . her voice sounded
    exquisitely as she spoke.

My mother looked in delight and amazement at the stranger,
She looked at the beauty of her tallborne face and full and
    pliant limbs,
The more she looked upon her she loved her,
Never before had she seen such wonderful beauty and purity;
She made her sit on a bench by the jamb of the
    fireplace . . . . she cooked food for her,
She had no work to give her but she gave her remembrance
    and fondness.

The red squaw staid all the forenoon, and toward the middle
    of the afternoon she went away;
O my mother was loth to have her go away,
All the week she thought of her . . . . she watched for her
    many a month,

She remembered her many a winter and many a summer,
But the red squaw never came nor was heard of there again.

Now Lucifer was not dead .... or if he was I am his sorrowful
    terrible heir;
I have been wronged .... I am oppressed .... I hate him that
    oppresses me,
I will either destroy him, or he shall release me.

Damn him! how he does defile me,
How he informs against my brother and sister and takes pay
    for their blood,
How he laughs when I look down the bend after the
    steamboat that carries away my woman.

Now the vast dusk bulk that is the whale's bulk .... it seems
    mine,
Warily, sportsman! though I lie so sleepy and sluggish, my
    tap is death.

[7]

A show of the summer softness .... a contact of something
    unseen .... an amour of the light and air;
I am jealous and overwhelmed with friendliness,
And will go gallivant with the light and the air myself,
And have an unseen something to be in contact with them
    also.

O love and summer! you are in the dreams and in me,
Autumn and winter are in the dreams .... the farmer goes
    with his thrift,
The droves and crops increase .... the barns are wellfilled.

Elements merge in the night . . . . ships make tacks in the
    dreams . . . . the sailor sails . . . . the exile returns home,
The fugitive returns unharmed . . . . the immigrant is back
    beyond months and years;
The poor Irishman lives in the simple house of his
    childhood, with the wellknown neighbors and faces,
They warmly welcome him . . . . he is barefoot again . . . . he
    forgets he is welloff;
The Dutchman voyages home, and the Scotchman and
    Welchman voyage home . . and the native of the
    Mediterranean voyages home;
To every port of England and France and Spain enter
    wellfilled ships;
The Swiss foots it toward his hills . . . . the Prussian goes his
    way, and the Hungarian his way, and the Pole goes his way,
The Swede returns, and the Dane and Norwegian return.

The homeward bound and the outward bound,
The beautiful lost swimmer, the ennuyee, the onanist, the
    female that loves unrequited, the moneymaker,
The actor and actress . . those through with their parts and
    those waiting to commence,
The affectionate boy, the husband and wife, the voter, the
    nominee that is chosen and the nominee that has failed,
The great already known, and the great anytime after to day,
The stammerer, the sick, the perfectformed, the homely,
The criminal that stood in the box, the judge that sat and
    sentenced him, the fluent lawyers, the jury, the audience,
The laugher and weeper, the dancer, the midnight widow, the
    red squaw,
The consumptive, the erysipalite, the idiot, he that is
    wronged,

The antipodes, and every one between this and them in the
    dark,
I swear they are averaged now . . . . one is no better than the
    other,
The night and sleep have likened them and restored them.

I swear they are all beautiful,
Every one that sleeps is beautiful . . . . every thing in the dim
    night is beautiful,
The wildest and bloodiest is over and all is peace.

Peace is always beautiful,
The myth of heaven indicates peace and night.

The myth of heaven indicates the soul;
The soul is always beautiful . . . . it appears more or it
    appears less . . . . it comes or lags behind,
It comes from its embowered garden and looks pleasantly on
    itself and encloses the world;
Perfect and clean the genitals previously jetting, and perfect
    and clean the womb cohering,
The head wellgrown and proportioned and plumb, and the
    bowels and joints proportioned and plumb.

The soul is always beautiful,
The universe is duly in order . . . . every thing is in its place,
What is arrived is in its place, and what waits is in its place;
The twisted skull waits . . . . the watery or rotten blood
    waits,
The child of the glutton or venerealee waits long, and the
    child of the drunkard waits long, and the drunkard
    himself waits long,

The sleepers that lived and died wait . . . . the far advanced
    are to go on in their turns, and the far behind are to go
    on in their turns,
The diverse shall be no less diverse, but they shall flow and
    unite . . . . they unite now.

[8]

The sleepers are very beautiful as they lie unclothed,
They flow hand in hand over the whole earth from east to
    west as they lie unclothed;
The Asiatic and African are hand in hand . . the European
    and American are hand in hand,
Learned and unlearned are hand in hand . . and male and
    female are hand in hand;
The bare arm of the girl crosses the bare breast of her
    lover . . . . they press close without lust . . . . his lips press
    her neck,
The father holds his grown or ungrown son in his arms with
    measureless love . . . . and the son holds the father in his
    arms with measureless love,
The white hair of the mother shines on the white wrist of the
    daughter,
The breath of the boy goes with the breath of the
    man . . . . friend is inarmed by friend,
The scholar kisses the teacher and the teacher kisses the
    scholar . . . . the wronged is made right,
The call of the slave is one with the master's call . . and the
    master salutes the slave,
The felon steps forth from the prison . . . . the insane
    becomes sane . . . . the suffering of sick persons is
    relieved,

The sweatings and fevers stop . . the throat that was unsound
    is sound . . the lungs of the consumptive are
    resumed . . the poor distressed head is free,
The joints of the rheumatic move as smoothly as ever, and
    smoother than ever,
Stiflings and passages open . . . . the paralysed become
    supple,
The swelled and convulsed and congested awake to
    themselves in condition,
They pass the invigoration of the night and the chemistry of
    the night and awake.

I too pass from the night;
I stay awhile away O night, but I return to you again and love
    you;
Why should I be afraid to trust myself to you?
I am not afraid . . . . I have been well brought forward by you;
I love the rich running day, but I do not desert her in whom I
    lay so long:
I know not how I came of you, and I know not where I go
    with you . . . . but I know I came well and shall go well.

I will stop only a time with the night . . . . and rise betimes.

I will duly pass the day O my mother and duly return to you;
Not you will yield forth the dawn again more surely than you
    will yield forth me again,
Not the womb yields the babe in its time more surely than I
    shall be yielded from you in my time.

LEAVES OF GRASS

[I Sing the Body Electric]

[1]

The bodies of men and women engirth me, and I engirth them,
They will not let me off nor I them till I go with them and
respond to them and love them.

Was it dreamed whether those who corrupted their own live
bodies could conceal themselves?
And whether those who defiled the living were as bad as
they who defiled the dead?

[2]

The expression of the body of man or woman balks account,
The male is perfect and that of the female is perfect.

The expression of a wellmade man appears not only in his
face,
It is in his limbs and joints also . . . . it is curiously in the
joints of his hips and wrists,
It is in his walk . . the carriage of his neck . . the flex of his
waist and knees . . . . dress does not hide him,
The strong sweet supple quality he has strikes through the
cotton and flannel;
To see him pass conveys as much as the best
poem . . perhaps more,

You linger to see his back and the back of his neck and
     shoulderside.
The sprawl and fulness of babes . . . . the bosoms and heads
     of women . . . . the folds of their dress . . . . their style as
     we pass in the street . . . . the contour of their shape
     downwards;
The swimmer naked in the swimmingbath . . seen as he
     swims through the salt transparent greenshine, or lies on
     his back and rolls silently with the heave of the water;
Framers bare-armed framing a house . . hoisting the beams in
     their places . . or using the mallet and mortising-chisel,
The bending forward and backward of rowers in
     rowboats . . . . the horseman in his saddle;
Girls and mothers and housekeepers in all their exquisite
     offices,
The group of laborers seated at noontime with their open
     dinner-kettles, and their wives waiting,
The female soothing a child . . . . the farmer's daughter in the
     garden or cowyard,
The woodman rapidly swinging his axe in the woods . . . . the
     young fellow hoeing corn . . . . the sleighdriver guiding
     his six horses through the crowd,
The wrestle of wrestlers . . . . two apprentice-boys, quite
     grown, lusty, goodnatured, nativeborn, out on the vacant
     lot at sundown after work,
The coats vests and caps thrown down . . the embrace of love
     and resistance,
The upperhold and underhold—the hair rumpled over and
     blinding the eyes;
The march of firemen in their own costumes—the play of the
     masculine muscle through cleansetting trowsers and
     waistbands,

The slow return from the fire .... the pause when the bell
    strikes suddenly again—the listening on the alert,
The natural perfect and varied attitudes .... the bent head,
    the curved neck, the counting:
Suchlike I love .... I loosen myself and pass freely .... and
    am at the mother's breast with the little child,
And swim with the swimmer, and wrestle with wrestlers, and
    march in line with the firemen, and pause and listen and
    count.

[3]

I knew a man .... he was a common farmer .... he was the
    father of five sons .... and in them were the fathers of
    sons .... and in them were the fathers of sons.

This man was a wonderful vigor and calmness and beauty of
    person;
The shape of his head, the richness and breadth of his
    manners, the pale yellow and white of his hair and
    beard, the immeasurable meaning of his black eyes,
These I used to go and visit him to see .... He was wise also,
He was six feet tall .... he was over eighty years old .... his
    sons were massive clean bearded tanfaced and handsome,
They and his daughters loved him ... all who saw him loved
    him ... they did not love him by allowance ... they loved
    him with personal love;
He drank water only .... the blood showed like scarlet
    through the clear brown skin of his face;
He was a frequent gunner and fisher ... he sailed his boat
    himself ... he had a fine one presented to him by a
    shipjoiner .... he had fowling pieces, presented to him
    by men that loved him;

When he went with his five sons and many grandsons to
      hunt or fish you would pick him out as the most
      beautiful and vigorous of the gang,
You would wish long and long to be with him . . . . you would
      wish to sit by him in the boat that you and he might
      touch each other.

[4]

I have perceived that to be with those I like is enough,
To stop in company with the rest at evening is enough,
To be surrounded by beautiful curious breathing laughing
      flesh is enough,
To pass among them . . to touch any one . . . . to rest my arm
      ever so lightly round his or her neck for a
      moment . . . . what is this then?
I do not ask any more delight . . . . I swim in it as in a sea.

There is something in staying close to men and women and
      looking on them and in the contact and odor of them that
      pleases the soul well,
All things please the soul, but these please the soul well.

[5]

This is the female form,
A divine nimbus exhales from it from head to foot,
It attracts with fierce undeniable attraction,
I am drawn by its breath as if I were no more than a helpless
      vapor . . . . all falls aside but myself and it,
Books, art, religion, time . . the visible and solid earth . .
      the atmosphere and the fringed clouds . . what was
      expected of heaven or feared of hell are now
      consumed,

Mad filaments, ungovernable shoots play out of it .. the
    response likewise ungovernable,
Hair, bosom, hips, bend of legs, negligent falling hands—all
    diffused . . . . mine too diffused,
Ebb stung by the flow, and flow stung by the
    ebb . . . . loveflesh swelling and deliciously aching,
Limitless limpid jets of love hot and enormous . . . . quivering
    jelly of love . . . . white-blow and delirious juice,
Bridegroom-night of love working surely and softly into the
    prostrate dawn,
Undulating into the willing and yielding day,
Lost in the cleave of the clasping and sweetfleshed day.

This is the nucleus . . . after the child is born of woman the
    man is born of woman,
This is the bath of birth . . . this is the merge of small and
    large and the outlet again.

Be not ashamed women .. your privilege encloses the
    rest .. it is the exit of the rest,
You are the gates of the body and you are the gates of the soul.

The female contains all qualities and tempers them . . . . she
    is in her place . . . . she moves with perfect balance,
She is all things duly veiled . . . . she is both passive and
    active . . . . she is to conceive daughters as well as sons
    and sons as well as daughters.

As I see my soul reflected in nature . . . . as I see through
    a mist one with inexpressible completeness and
    beauty . . . . see the bent head and arms folded over the
    breast . . . . the female I see,

I see the bearer of the great fruit which is immortality . . . .
     the good thereof is not tasted by roues, and never can be.

[6]

The male is not less the soul, nor more . . . . he too is in his
     place,
He too is all qualities . . . . he is action and power . . . . the
     flush of the known universe is in him,
Scorn becomes him well and appetite and defiance become
     him well,
The fiercest largest passions . . bliss that is utmost and sorrow
     that is utmost become him well . . . . pride is for him,
The fullspread pride of man is calming and excellent to the
     soul;
Knowledge becomes him . . . . he likes it always . . . . he brings
     everything to the test of himself,
Whatever the survey . . whatever the sea and the sail, he
     strikes soundings at last only here,
Where else does he strike soundings except here?

The man's body is sacred and the woman's body is
     sacred . . . . it is no matter who,
Is it a slave? Is it one of the dullfaced immigrants just landed
     on the wharf?

Each belongs here or anywhere just as much as the
     welloff . . . . just as much as you,
Each has his or her place in the procession.

All is a procession,
The universe is a procession with measured and beautiful
     motion.

Do you know so much that you call the slave or the dullfaced
ignorant?
Do you suppose you have a right to a good sight . . . and he or
she has no right to a sight?
Do you think matter has cohered together from its diffused
float, and the soil is on the surface and water runs and
vegetation sprouts for you . . and not for him and her?

[7]

A slave at auction!
I help the auctioneer . . . . the sloven does not half know his
business.

Gentlemen look on this curious creature,
Whatever the bids of the bidders they cannot be high enough
for him,
For him the globe lay preparing quintillions of years without
one animal or plant,
For him the revolving cycles truly and steadily rolled.

In that head the allbaffling brain,
In it and below it the making of the attributes of heroes.

Examine these limbs, red black or white . . . . they are very
cunning in tendon and nerve;
They shall be stript that you may see them.

Exquisite senses, lifelit eyes, pluck, volition,
Flakes of breastmuscle, pliant backbone and neck, flesh not
flabby, goodsized arms and legs,
And wonders within there yet.

Within there runs his blood . . . . the same old blood . . the
    same red running blood;
There swells and jets his heart . . . . There all passions and
    desires . . all reachings and aspirations:
Do you think they are not there because they are not
    expressed in parlors and lecture-rooms?

This is not only one man . . . . he is the father of those who
    shall be fathers in their turns,
In him the start of populous states and rich republics,
Of him countless immortal lives with countless embodiments
    and enjoyments.

How do you know who shall come from the offspring of his
    offspring through the centuries?
Who might you find you have come from yourself if you
    could trace back through the centuries?

[8]

A woman at auction,
She too is not only herself . . . . she is the teeming mother of
    mothers,
She is the bearer of them that shall grow and be mates to the
    mothers.

Her daughters or their daughters' daughters . . who knows
    who shall mate with them?
Who knows through the centuries what heroes may come
    from them?

In them and of them natal love . . . . in them the divine
    mystery . . . . the same old beautiful mystery.

Have you ever loved a woman?
Your mother . . . . is she living? . . . . Have you been much with
    her? and has she been much with you?
Do you not see that these are exactly the same to all in all
    nations and times all over the earth?

If life and the soul are sacred the human body is sacred;
And the glory and sweet of a man is the token of manhood
    untainted,
And in man or woman a clean strong firmfibred body is
    beautiful as the most beautiful face.

Have you seen the fool that corrupted his own live body? or
    the fool that corrupted her own live body?
For they do not conceal themselves, and cannot conceal
    themselves.

Who degrades or defiles the living human body is cursed,
Who degrades or defiles the body of the dead is not more
    cursed.

LEAVES OF GRASS

[Faces]

[1]

Sauntering the pavement or riding the country byroads here
    then are faces,
Faces of friendship, precision, caution, sauvity, ideality,
The spiritual prescient face, the always welcome common
    benevolent face,
The face of the singing of music, the grand faces of natural
    lawyers and judges broad at the backtop,
The faces of hunters and fishers, bulged at the brows .... the
    shaved blanched faces of orthodox citizens,
The pure extravagant yearning questioning artist's face,
The welcome ugly face of some beautiful soul .... the
    handsome detested or despised face,
The sacred faces of infants .... the illuminated face of the
    mother of many children,
The face of an amour .... the face of veneration,
The face as of a dream .... the face of an immobile
    rock,
The face withdrawn of its good and bad .. a castrated
    face,
A wild hawk .. his wings clipped by the clipper,
A stallion that yielded at last to the thongs and knife of the
    gelder.

Sauntering the pavement or crossing the ceaseless ferry,
　　here then are faces;
I see them and complain not and am content with all.

[2]

Do you suppose I could be content with all if I thought them
　　their own finale?
This now is too lamentable a face for a man;
Some abject louse asking leave to be . . cringing for it,
Some milknosed maggot blessing what lets it wrig to its
　　hole.

This face is a dog's snout sniffing for garbage;
Snakes nest in that mouth . . I hear the sibilant threat.

This face is a haze more chill than the arctic sea,
Its sleepy and wobbling icebergs crunch as they go.

This is a face of bitter herbs . . . . this an emetic . . . . they
　　need no label,
And more of the drugshelf . . laudanum, caoutchouc, or hog's
　　lard.

This face is an epilepsy advertising and doing business . . . . its
　　wordless tongue gives out the unearthly cry,
Its veins down the neck distend . . . . its eyes roll till they
　　show nothing but their whites,
Its teeth grit . . the palms of the hands are cut by the
　　turned-in nails,
The man falls struggling and foaming to the ground while he
　　speculates well.

This face is bitten by vermin and worms,
And this is some murderer's knife with a halfpulled
scabbard.

This face owes to the sexton his dismalest fee,
An unceasing deathbell tolls there.

Those are really men! . . . . the bosses and tufts of the great
round globe!

[3]

Features of my equals, would you trick me with your creased
and cadaverous march?
Well then you cannot trick me.

I see your rounded never-erased flow,
I see neath the rims of your haggard and mean disguises.

Splay and twist as you like . . . . poke with the tangling fores
of fishes or rats,
You'll be unmuzzled . . . . you certainly will.

I saw the face of the most smeared and slobbering idiot they
had at the asylum,
And I knew for my consolation what they knew not;
I knew of the agents that emptied and broke my brother,
The same wait to clear the rubbish from the fallen
tenement;
And I shall look again in a score or two of ages,
And I shall meet the real landlord perfect and unharmed,
every inch as good as myself.

[4]

The Lord advances and yet advances:
Always the shadow in front . . . . always the reached hand
    bringing up the laggards.

Out of this face emerge banners and horses . . . . O
    superb! . . . . I see what is coming,
I see the high pioneercaps . . . . I see the staves of runners
    clearing the way,
I hear victorious drums.

This face is a lifeboat;
This is the face commanding and bearded . . . . it asks no
    odds of the rest;
This face is flavored fruit ready for eating;
This face of a healthy honest boy is the programme of all good.

These faces bear testimony slumbering or awake,
They show their descent from the Master himself.

Off the word I have spoken I except not one . . . . red white or
    black, all are deific,
In each house is the ovum . . . . it comes forth after a
    thousand years.

Spots or cracks at the windows do not disturb me,
Tall and sufficient stand behind and make signs to me;
I read the promise and patiently wait.

This is a fullgrown lily's face,
She speaks to the limber-hip'd man near the garden pickets,

Come here, she blushingly cries . . . . Come nigh to me
    limber-hip'd man and give me your finger and
    thumb,
Stand at my side till I lean as high as I can upon you,
Fill me with albescent honey . . . . bend down to me,
Rub to me with your chafing beard . . rub to my breast and
    shoulders.

[5]

The old face of the mother of many children:
Whist! I am fully content.

Lulled and late is the smoke of the Sabbath
    morning,
It hangs low over the rows of trees by the
    fences,
It hangs thin by the sassafras, the wildcherry and the
    catbrier under them.

I saw the rich ladies in full dress at the soiree,
I heard what the run of poets were saying so long,
Heard who sprang in crimson youth from the white froth and
    the water-blue.

Behold a woman!
She looks out from her quaker cap . . . . her face is clearer
    and more beautiful than the sky.

She sits in an armchair under the shaded porch of the
    farmhouse,
The sun just shines on her old white head.

Her ample gown is of creamhued linen,
Her grandsons raised the flax, and her granddaughters spun
    it with the distaff and the wheel.

The melodious character of the earth!
The finish beyond which philosophy cannot go and does not
    wish to go!
The justified mother of men!

[Song of the Answerer]

A young man came to me with a message from his brother,
How should the young man know the whether and when of
    his brother?
Tell him to send me the signs.

And I stood before the young man face to face, and took his
    right hand in my left hand and his left hand in my right
    hand,
And I answered for his brother and for men . . . . and I
    answered for the poet, and sent these signs.

Him all wait for . . . . him all yield up to . . . . his word is
    decisive and final,
Him they accept . . . . in him lave . . . . in him perceive
    themselves as amid light,
Him they immerse, and he immerses them.

Beautiful women, the haughtiest nations, laws, the landscape,
    people and animals,
The profound earth and its attributes, and the unquiet
    ocean,
All enjoyments and properties, and money, and whatever
    money will buy,

The best farms .... others toiling and planting, and he
　　unavoidably reaps,
The noblest and costliest cities .... others grading and
　　building, and he domiciles there;
Nothing for any one but what is for him .... near and far are
　　for him,
The ships in the offing .... the perpetual shows and marches
　　on land are for him if they are for any body.

He puts things in their attitudes,
He puts today out of himself with plasticity and love,
He places his own city, times, reminiscences, parents,
　　brothers and sisters, associations employment and
　　politics, so that the rest never shame them afterward, nor
　　assume to command them.

He is the answerer,
What can be answered he answers, and what cannot be
　　answered he shows how it cannot be answered.

A man is a summons and challenge,
It is vain to skulk .... Do you hear that mocking and
　　laughter? Do you hear the ironical echoes?

Books friendships philosophers priests action pleasure pride
　　beat up and down seeking to give satisfaction;
He indicates the satisfaction, and indicates them that beat up
　　and down also.

Whichever the sex ... whatever the season or place he
　　may go freshly and gently and safely by day or by
　　night,

He has the passkey of hearts . . . . to him the response of the
    prying of hands on the knobs.

His welcome is universal . . . . the flow of beauty is not more
    welcome or universal than he is,
The person he favors by day or sleeps with at night is blessed.

Every existence has its idiom . . . . every thing has an idiom
    and tongue;
He resolves all tongues into his own, and bestows it upon
    men . . and any man translates . . and any man translates
    himself also:
One part does not counteract another part . . . . He is the
    joiner . . he sees how they join.

He says indifferently and alike, How are you friend? to the
    President at his levee,
And he says Good day my brother, to Cudge that hoes in the
    sugarfield;
And both understand him and know that his speech is right.

He walks with perfect ease in the capitol,
He walks among the Congress . . . . and one representative
    says to another, Here is our equal appearing and new.

Then the mechanics take him for a mechanic,
And the soldiers suppose him to be a captain . . . . and the
    sailors that he has followed the sea,
And the authors take him for an author . . . . and the artists
    for an artist,
And the laborers perceive he could labor with them and love
    them;

No matter what the work is, that he is one to follow it or has
    followed it,
No matter what the nation, that he might find his brothers
    and sisters there.

The English believe he comes of their English stock,
A Jew to the Jew he seems .... a Russ to the Russ .... usual
    and near .. removed from none.

Whoever he looks at in the traveler's coffeehouse claims him,
The Italian or Frenchman is sure, and the German is sure, and
    the Spaniard is sure .... and the island Cuban is sure.

The engineer, the deckhand on the great lakes or on the
    Mississippi or St. Lawrence or Sacramento or Hudson or
    Delaware claims him.

The gentleman of perfect blood acknowledges his perfect
    blood,
The insulter, the prostitute, the angry person, the beggar, see
    themselves in the ways of him .... he strangely
    transmutes them,
They are not vile any more .... they hardly know themselves,
    they are so grown.

You think it would be good to be the writer of melodious verses,
Well it would be good to be the writer of melodious verses;
But what are verses beyond the flowing character you could
    have? .... or beyond beautiful manners and behaviour?
Or beyond one manly or affectionate deed of an
    apprenticeboy? .... or old woman? .. or man that has
    been in prison or is likely to be in prison?

[Europe: The 72d and 73d Years of These States]

Suddenly out of its stale and drowsy lair, the lair of slaves,
Like lightning Europe le'pt forth . . . . half startled at itself,
Its feet upon the ashes and the rags . . . . Its hands tight to the
throats of kings.

O hope and faith! O aching close of lives! O many a sickened
heart!
Turn back unto this day, and make yourselves afresh.

And you, paid to defile the People . . . . you liars mark:
Not for numberless agonies, murders, lusts,
For court thieving in its manifold mean forms,
Worming from his simplicity the poor man's wages;
For many a promise sworn by royal lips, and broken, and
laughed at in the breaking,
Then in their power not for all these did the blows strike of
personal revenge . . or the heads of the nobles fall;
The People scorned the ferocity of kings.

But the sweetness of mercy brewed bitter destruction, and
the frightened rulers come back:
Each comes in state with his train . . . . hangman, priest and
tax-gatherer . . . . soldier, lawyer, jailer and sycophant.

Yet behind all, lo, a Shape,
Vague as the night, draped interminably, head front and form
    in scarlet folds,
Whose face and eyes none may see,
Out of its robes only this .... the red robes, lifted by the arm,
One finger pointed high over the top, like the head of a snake
    appears.
Meanwhile corpses lie in new-made graves .... bloody
    corpses of young men:
The rope of the gibbet hangs heavily .... the bullets of
    princes are flying .... the creatures of power laugh
    aloud,
And all these things bear fruits .... and they are good.

Those corpses of young men,
Those martyrs that hang from the gibbets ... those hearts
    pierced by the gray lead,
Cold and motionless as they seem .. live elsewhere with
    unslaughter'd vitality.

They live in other young men, O kings,
They live in brothers, again ready to defy you:
They were purified by death .... they were taught and
    exalted.

Not a grave of the murdered for freedom but grows seed for
    freedom .... in its turn to bear seed,
Which the winds carry afar and re-sow, and the rains and the
    snows nourish.

Not a disembodied spirit can the weapons of tyrants let
    loose,

But it stalks invisibly over the earth . . whispering counseling
    cautioning.

Liberty let others despair of you . . . . I never despair of you.

Is the house shut? Is the master away?
Nevertheless be ready . . . . be not weary of watching,
He will soon return . . . . his messengers come anon.

[A Boston Ballad]

Clear the way there Jonathan!
Way for the President's marshal! Way for the government
    cannon!
Way for the federal foot and dragoons . . . . and the phantoms
    afterward.

I rose this morning early to get betimes in Boston town;
Here's a good place at the corner . . . . I must stand and see
    the show.

I love to look on the stars and stripes . . . . I hope the fifes will
    play Yankee Doodle.

How bright shine the foremost with cutlasses,
Every man holds his revolver . . . . marching stiff through
    Boston town.

A fog follows . . . . antiques of the same come limping,
Some appear wooden-legged and some appear bandaged
    and bloodless.

Why this is a show! It has called the dead out of the earth,
The old graveyards of the hills have hurried to see;

Uncountable phantoms gather by flank and rear of it,
Cocked hats of mothy mould and crutches made of mist,
Arms in slings and old men leaning on young men's
    shoulders.

What troubles you, Yankee phantoms? What is all this
    chattering of bare gums?
Does the ague convulse your limbs? Do you mistake your
    crutches for firelocks, and level them?
If you blind your eyes with tears you will not see the
    President's marshal,
If you groan such groans you might balk the government
    cannon.

For shame old maniacs! .... Bring down those tossed arms,
    and let your white hair be;
Here gape your smart grandsons .... their wives gaze at
    them from the windows,
See how well-dressed .... see how orderly they conduct
    themselves.

Worse and worse .... Can't you stand it? Are you retreating?
Is this hour with the living too dead for you?

Retreat then! Pell-mell! .... Back to the hills, old limpers!
I do not think you belong here anyhow.

But there is one thing that belongs here .... Shall I tell you
    what it is, gentlemen of Boston?

I will whisper it to the Mayor .... he shall send a committee
    to England,

They shall get a grant from the Parliament, and go with a
    cart to the royal vault.
Dig out King George's coffin . . . . unwrap him quick from the
    graveclothes . . . . box up his bones for a journey:
Find a swift Yankee clipper . . . . here is freight for you
    blackbellied clipper,
Up with your anchor! shake out your sails! . . . . steer straight
    toward Boston bay.

Now call the President's marshal again, and bring out the
    government cannon,
And fetch home the roarers from Congress, and make
    another procession and guard it with foot and dragoons.

Here is a centrepiece for them:
Look! all orderly citizens . . . . look from the windows women.

The committee open the box and set up the regal ribs and
    glue those that will not stay,
And clap the skull on top of the ribs, and clap a crown on top
    of the skull.

You have got your revenge old buster! . . . . The crown is come
    to its own and more than its own.

Stick your hands in your pockets Jonathan . . . . you are a
    made man from this day,
You are mighty cute . . . . and here is one of your bargains.

[There Was a Child Went Forth]

There was a child went forth every day,
And the first object he looked upon and received with
    wonder or pity or love or dread, that object he became,
And that object became part of him for the day or a certain
    part of the day . . . . or for many years or stretching cycles
    of years.

The early lilacs became part of this child,
And grass, and white and red morningglories, and white and
    red clover, and the song of the phœbe-bird,
And the March-born lambs, and the sow's pink-faint litter, and
    the mare's foal, and the cow's calf, and the noisy brood of
    the barnyard or by the mire of the pondside . . and the fish
    suspending themselves so curiously below there . . and
    the beautiful curious liquid . . and the water-plants with
    their graceful flat heads . . all became part of him.

And the field-sprouts of April and May became part of
    him . . . . wintergrain sprouts, and those of the light-
    yellow corn, and of the esculent roots of the garden,
And the appletrees covered with blossoms, and the fruit
    afterward . . . . and woodberries . . and the commonest
    weeds by the road;

And the old drunkard staggering home from the outhouse of
    the tavern whence he had lately risen,
And the schoolmistress that passed on her way to the
    school . . and the friendly boys that passed . . and the
    quarrelsome boys . . and the tidy and freshcheeked
    girls . . and the barefoot negro boy and girl,
And all the changes of city and country wherever he went.

His own parents . . he that had propelled the fatherstuff at
    night, and fathered him . . and she that conceived him in
    her womb and birthed him . . . . they gave this child more
    of themselves than that,
They gave him afterward every day . . . . they and of them
    became part of him.

The mother at home quietly placing the dishes on the
    suppertable,
The mother with mild words . . . . clean her cap and
    gown . . . . a wholesome odor falling off her person and
    clothes as she walks by:
The father, strong, selfsufficient, manly, mean, angered,
    unjust,
The blow, the quick loud word, the tight bargain, the crafty
    lure,
The family usages, the language, the company, the
    furniture . . . . the yearning and swelling heart,
Affection that will not be gainsayed . . . . The sense of what is
    real . . . . the thought if after all it should prove unreal,
The doubts of daytime and the doubts of nighttime . . . the
    curious whether and how,
Whether that which appears so is so . . . . Or is it all flashes
    and specks?

Men and women crowding fast in the streets .. if they are not
  flashes and specks what are they?
The streets themselves, and the facades of houses .... the
  goods in the windows,
Vehicles .. teams .. the tiered wharves, and the huge crossing
  at the ferries;
The village on the highland seen from afar at sunset .... the
  river between,
Shadows .. aureola and mist .. light falling on roofs and
  gables of white or brown, three miles off,
The schooner near by sleepily dropping down the tide .. the
  little boat slacktowed astern,
The hurrying tumbling waves and quickbroken crests and
  slapping;
The strata of colored clouds .... the long bar of maroontint
  away solitary by itself .... the spread of purity it lies
  motionless in,
The horizon's edge, the flying seacrow, the fragrance of
  saltmarsh and shoremud;
These became part of that child who went forth every day,
  and who now goes and will always go forth every day,
And these become of him or her that peruses them now.

[Who Learns My Lesson Complete?]

Who learns my lesson complete?
Boss and journeyman and apprentice? . . . . churchman and
    atheist?
The stupid and the wise thinker . . . . parents and
    offspring . . . . merchant and clerk and porter and
    customer . . . . editor, author, artist and schoolboy?

Draw nigh and commence,
It is no lesson . . . . it lets down the bars to a good lesson,
And that to another . . . . and every one to another still.

The great laws take and effuse without argument,
I am of the same style, for I am their friend,
I love them quits and quits . . . . I do not halt and make
    salaams.

I lie abstracted and hear beautiful tales of things and the
    reasons of things,
They are so beautiful I nudge myself to listen.

I cannot say to any person what I hear . . . . I cannot say it to
    myself . . . . it is very wonderful.

It is no little matter, this round and delicious globe, moving
    so exactly in its orbit forever and ever, without one jolt or
    the untruth of a single second;
I do not think it was made in six days, nor in ten thousand
    years, nor ten decillions of years,
Nor planned and built one thing after another, as an
    architect plans and builds a house.

I do not think seventy years is the time of a man or woman,
Nor that seventy millions of years is the time of a man or
    woman,
Nor that years will ever stop the existence of me or any one
    else.
Is it wonderful that I should be immortal? as every one is
    immortal,
I know it is wonderful .... but my eyesight is equally
    wonderful .... and how I was conceived in my mother's
    womb is equally wonderful,
And how I was not palpable once but am now .... and was
    born on the last day of May 1819 .... and passed from a
    babe in the creeping trance of three summers and three
    winters to articulate and walk .... are all equally
    wonderful.

And that I grew six feet high .... and that I have become a
    man thirty-six years old in 1855 .... and that I am here
    anyhow—are all equally wonderful;
And that my soul embraces you this hour, and we affect each
    other without ever seeing each other, and never perhaps
    to see each other, is every bit as wonderful:
And that I can think such thoughts as these is just as
    wonderful,

And that I can remind you, and you think them and know
    them to be true is just as wonderful,
And that the moon spins round the earth and on with the
    earth is equally wonderful,
And that they balance themselves with the sun and stars is
    equally wonderful.

Come I should like to hear you tell me what there is in
    yourself that is not just as wonderful,
And I should like to hear the name of anything between
    Sunday morning and Saturday night that is not just as
    wonderful.

[Great Are the Myths]

[1]

Great are the myths .... I too delight in them,

Great are Adam and Eve .... I too look back and accept
them;

Great the risen and fallen nations, and their poets, women,
sages, inventors, rulers, warriors and priests.

Great is liberty! Great is equality! I am their follower,

Helmsmen of nations, choose your craft .... where you sail I
sail,

Yours is the muscle of life or death .... yours is the perfect
science .... in you I have absolute faith.

Great is today, and beautiful,

It is good to live in this age .... there never was any better.

Great are the plunges and throes and triumphs and falls of
democracy,

Great the reformers with their lapses and screams,

Great the daring and venture of sailors on new explorations.

Great are yourself and myself,

We are just as good and bad as the oldest and youngest or
any,

What the best and worst did we could do,
What they felt .. do not we feel it in ourselves?
What they wished .. do we not wish the same?

Great is youth, and equally great is old age .... great are the
     day and night;
Great is wealth and great is poverty .... great is expression
     and great is silence.

Youth large lusty and loving .... youth full of grace and force
     and fascination,
Do you know that old age may come after you with equal
     grace and force and fascination?

Day fullblown and splendid .... day of the immense sun, and
     action and ambition and laughter,
The night follows close, with millions of suns, and sleep and
     restoring darkness.

Wealth with the flush hand and fine clothes and
     hospitality:
But then the soul's wealth—which is candor and knowledge
     and pride and enfolding love:
Who goes for men and women showing poverty richer than
     wealth?

Expression of speech .. in what is written or said forget not
     that silence is also expressive,
That anguish as hot as the hottest and contempt as cold as
     the coldest may be without words,
That the true adoration is likewise without words and
     without kneeling.

[2]

Great is the greatest nation . . the nation of clusters of equal
    nations.

Great is the earth, and the way it became what it is,
Do you imagine it is stopped at this? . . . . and the increase
    abandoned?
Understand then that it goes as far onward from this as this is
    from the times when it lay in covering waters and gases.

Great is the quality of truth in man,
The quality of truth in man supports itself through all changes,
It is inevitably in the man . . . . He and it are in love, and
    never leave each other.

The truth in man is no dictum . . . . it is vital as eyesight,
If there be any soul there is truth . . . . if there be man or
    woman there is truth . . . . If there be physical or moral
    there is truth,
If there be equilibrium or volition there is truth . . . . if there
    be things at all upon the earth there is truth.

O truth of the earth! O truth of things! I am determined to
    press the whole way toward you,
Sound your voice! I scale mountains or dive in the sea after
    you.

[3]

Great is language . . . . it is the mightiest of the sciences,
It is the fulness and color and form and diversity of the
    earth . . . . and of men and women . . . . and of all qualities
    and processes;

It is greater than wealth .... it is greater than buildings or
    ships or religions or paintings or music.

Great is the English speech .... What speech is so great as
    the English?
Great is the English brood .... What brood has so vast a
    destiny as the English?
It is the mother of the brood that must rule the earth with
    the new rule,
The new rule shall rule as the soul rules, and as the love and
    justice and equality that are in the soul rule.

Great is the law .... Great are the old few landmarks of the
    law .... they are the same in all times and shall not be
    disturbed.
Great are marriage, commerce, newspapers, books, freetrade,
    railroads, steamers, international mails and telegraphs
    and exchanges.

[4]

Great is Justice;
Justice is not settled by legislators and laws .... it is in the
    soul,
It cannot be varied by statutes any more than love or pride or
    the attraction of gravity can,
It is immutable .. it does not depend on
    majorities .... majorities or what not come at last before
    the same passionless and exact tribunal.

For justice are the grand natural lawyers and perfect
    judges .... it is in their souls,

It is well assorted . . . . they have not studied for nothing . . . .
    the great includes the less,
They rule on the highest grounds . . . . they oversee all eras
    and states and administrations,

The perfect judge fears nothing . . . . he could go front to
    front before God,
Before the perfect judge all shall stand back . . . . life and
    death shall stand back . . . . heaven and hell shall stand
    back.

[5]

Great is goodness;
I do not know what it is any more than I know what health
    is . . . . but I know it is great.

Great is wickedness . . . . I find I often admire it just as much
    as I admire goodness:
Do you call that a paradox? It certainly is a paradox.

The eternal equilibrium of things is great, and the eternal
    overthrow of things is great,
And there is another paradox.

Great is life . . and real and mystical . . wherever and
    whoever,
Great is death . . . . Sure as life holds all parts together, death
    holds all parts together;
Sure as the stars return again after they merge in the light,
    death is great as life.

🌿🌿 1856 🌿🌿

CROSSING
BROOKLYN FERRY.

1

Flood-tide below me! I see you face to face!
Clouds of the west—sun there half an hour high—I see you
    also face to face.

Crowds of men and women attired in the usual costumes,
    how curious you are to me!
On the ferry-boats the hundreds and hundreds that cross,
    returning home, are more curious to me than you
    suppose,
And you that shall cross from shore to shore years hence are
    more to me, and more in my meditations, than you might
    suppose.

2

The impalpable sustenance of me from all things at all hours
    of the day,
The simple, compact, well-join'd scheme, myself
    disintegrated, every one disintegrated yet part of the
    scheme,
The similitudes of the past and those of the future,
The glories strung like beads on my smallest sights and
    hearings, on the walk in the street and the passage over
    the river,

The current rushing so swiftly and swimming with me far
    away,
The others that are to follow me, the ties between me and
    them,
The certainty of others, the life, love, sight, hearing of others.

Others will enter the gates of the ferry and cross from shore
    to shore,
Others will watch the run of the flood-tide,
Others will see the shipping of Manhattan north and west,
    and the heights of Brooklyn to the south and east,
Others will see the islands large and small;
Fifty years hence, others will see them as they cross, the sun
    half an hour high,
A hundred years hence, or ever so many hundred years
    hence, others will see them,
Will enjoy the sunset, the pouring-in of the flood-tide, the
    falling-back to the sea of the ebb-tide.

3

It avails not, time nor place—distance avails not,
I am with you, you men and women of a generation, or ever
    so many generations hence,
Just as you feel when you look on the river and sky, so I felt,
Just as any of you is one of a living crowd, I was one of a
    crowd,
Just as you are refresh'd by the gladness of the river and the
    bright flow, I was refresh'd,
Just as you stand and lean on the rail, yet hurry with the
    swift current, I stood yet was hurried,
Just as you look on the numberless masts of ships and the
    thick-stemm'd pipes of steamboats, I look'd.

I too many and many a time cross'd the river of old,
Watched the Twelfth-month sea-gulls, saw them high in the
    air floating with motionless wings, oscillating their bodies,
Saw how the glistening yellow lit up parts of their bodies and
    left the rest in strong shadow,
Saw the slow-wheeling circles and the gradual edging
    toward the south,
Saw the reflection of the summer sky in the water,
Had my eyes dazzled by the shimmering track of beams,
Look'd at the fine centrifugal spokes of light round the shape
    of my head in the sunlit water,
Look'd on the haze on the hills southward and south-westward,
Look'd on the vapor as it flew in fleeces tinged with violet,
Look'd toward the lower bay to notice the vessels arriving,
Saw their approach, saw abroad those that were near me,
Saw the white sails of schooners and sloops, saw the ships at
    anchor,
The sailors at work in the rigging or out astride the spars,
The round masts, the swinging motion of the hulls, the
    slender serpentine pennants,
The large and small steamers in motion, the pilots in their
    pilot-houses,
The white wake left by the passage, the quick tremulous
    whirl of the wheels,
The flags of all nations, the falling of them at sunset,
The scallop-edged waves in the twilight, the ladled cups, the
    frolicsome crests and glistening,
The stretch afar growing dimmer and dimmer, the gray walls
    of the granite storehouses by the docks,
On the river the shadowy group, the big steam-tug closely
    flank'd on each side by the barges, the hay-boat, the
    belated lighter,

On the neighboring shore the fires from the foundry
    chimneys burning high and glaringly into the night,
Casting their flicker of black contrasted with wild red and
    yellow light over the tops of houses, and down into the
    clefts of streets.

4

These and all else were to me the same as they are to you,
I loved well those cities, loved well the stately and rapid
    river,
The men and women I saw were all near to me,
Others the same—others who look back on me because I
    look'd forward to them,
(The time will come, though I stop here to-day and to-night.)

5

What is it then between us?
What is the count of the scores or hundreds of years
    between us?

Whatever it is, it avails not—distance avails not, and place
    avails not,
I too lived, Brooklyn of ample hills was mine,
I too walk'd the streets of Manhattan island, and bathed in
    the waters around it,
I too felt curious abrupt questionings stir within me,
In the day among crowds of people sometimes they came
    upon me,
In my walks home late at night or as I lay in my bed they
    came upon me,
I too had been struck from the float forever held in solution,
I too had receiv'd identity by my body,

That I was I knew was of my body, and what I should be I
    knew I should be of my body.

6

It is not upon you alone the dark patches fall,
The dark threw its patches down upon me also,
The best I had done seem'd to me blank and suspicious,
My great thoughts as I supposed them, were they not in
    reality meagre?
Nor is it you alone who know what it is to be evil,
I am he who knew what it was to be evil,
I too knitted the old knot of contrariety,
Blabb'd, blush'd, resented, lied, stole, grudg'd,
Had guile, anger, lust, hot wishes I dared not speak,
Was wayward, vain, greedy, shallow, sly, cowardly,
    malignant,
The wolf, the snake, the hog, not wanting in me,
The cheating look, the frivolous word, the adulterous wish,
    not wanting,
Refusals, hates, postponements, meanness, laziness, none of
    these wanting,
Was one with the rest, the days and haps of the rest,
Was call'd by my nighest name by clear loud voices of young
    men as they saw me approaching or passing,
Felt their arms on my neck as I stood, or the negligent
    leaning of their flesh against me as I sat,
Saw many I loved in the street or ferry-boat or public
    assembly, yet never told them a word,
Lived the same life with the rest, the same old laughing,
    gnawing, sleeping,
Play'd the part that still looks back on the actor or
    actress,

The same old role, the role that is what we make it, as great
    as we like,
Or as small as we like, or both great and small.

7

Closer yet I approach you,
What thought you have of me now, I had as much of you—I
    laid in my stores in advance,
I consider'd long and seriously of you before you were born.

Who was to know what should come home to me?
Who knows but I am enjoying this?
Who knows, for all the distance, but I am as good as looking
    at you now, for all you cannot see me?

8

Ah, what can ever be more stately and admirable to me than
    mast-hemm'd Manhattan?
River and sunset and scallop-edg'd waves of flood-tide?
The sea-gulls oscillating their bodies, the hay-boat in the
    twilight, and the belated lighter?
What gods can exceed these that clasp me by the hand, and
    with voices I love call me promptly and loudly by my
    nighest name as I approach?
What is more subtle than this which ties me to the woman or
    man that looks in my face?
Which fuses me into you now, and pours my meaning into
    you?

We understand then do we not?
What I promis'd without mentioning it, have you not accepted?

What the study could not teach—what the preaching could
    not accomplish is accomplish'd, is it not?

9

Flow on, river! flow with the flood-tide, and ebb with the
    ebb-tide!
Frolic on, crested and scallop-edg'd waves!
Gorgeous clouds of the sunset! drench with your splendor
    me, or the men and women generations after me!
Cross from shore to shore, countless crowds of passengers!
Stand up, tall masts of Mannahatta! stand up, beautiful hills
    of Brooklyn!
Throb, baffled and curious brain! throw out questions and
    answers!
Suspend here and everywhere, eternal float of solution!
Gaze, loving and thirsting eyes, in the house or street or
    public assembly!
Sound out, voices of young men! loudly and musically call
    me by my nighest name!
Live, old life! play the part that looks back on the actor and
    actress!
Play the old role, the role that is great or small according as
    one makes it!
Consider, you who peruse me, whether I may not in unknown
    ways be looking upon you;
Be firm, rail over the river, to support those who lean idly, yet
    haste with the hasting current;
Fly on, sea-birds! fly sideways, or wheel in large circles high
    in the air;
Receive the summer sky, you water, and faithfully hold it till
    all downcast eyes have time to take it from you!

Diverge, fine spokes of light, from the shape of my head, or
    any one's head, in the sunlit water!
Come on, ships from the lower bay! pass up or down, white-
    sail'd schooners, sloops, lighters!
Flaunt away, flags of all nations! be duly lower'd at sunset!
Burn high your fires, foundry chimneys! cast black shadows
    at nightfall! cast red and yellow light over the tops of the
    houses!
Appearances, now or henceforth, indicate what you are,
You necessary film, continue to envelop the soul,
About my body for me, and your body for you, be hung out
    divinest aromas,
Thrive, cities—bring your freight, bring your shows, ample
    and sufficient rivers,
Expand, being than which none else is perhaps more
    spiritual,
Keep your places, objects than which none else is more
    lasting.

You have waited, you always wait, you dumb, beautiful
    ministers,
We receive you with free sense at last, and are insatiate
    hence-forward,
Not you any more shall be able to foil us, or withhold
    yourselves from us,
We use you, and do not cast you aside—we plant you
    permanently within us,
We fathom you not—we love you—there is perfection in you
    also,
You furnish your parts toward eternity,
Great or small, you furnish your parts toward the soul.

SPONTANEOUS ME.

Spontaneous me, Nature,
The loving day, the mounting sun, the friend I am happy
    with,
The arm of my friend hanging idly over my shoulder,
The hillside whiten'd with blossoms of the mountain ash,
The same late in autumn, the hues of red, yellow, drab,
    purple, and light and dark green,
The rich coverlet of the grass, animals and birds, the private
    untrimm'd bank, the primitive apples, the pebble-stones,
Beautiful dripping fragments, the negligent list of one after
    another as I happen to call them to me or think of them,
The real poems, (what we call poems being merely pictures,)
The poems of the privacy of the night, and of men like me,
This poem drooping shy and unseen that I always carry, and
    that all men carry,
(Know once for all, avow'd on purpose, wherever are men
    like me, are our lusty lurking masculine poems,)
Love-thoughts, love-juice, love-odor, love-yielding, love-
    climbers, and the climbing sap,
Arms and hands of love, lips of love, phallic thumb of love,
    breasts of love, bellies press'd and glued together with
    love,
Earth of chaste love, life that is only life after love,

The body of my love, the body of the woman I love, the body
     of the man, the body of the earth,
Soft forenoon airs that blow from the south-west,
The hairy wild-bee that murmurs and hankers up and down,
     that gripes the full-grown lady-flower, curves upon her
     with amorous firm legs, takes his will of her, and holds
     himself tremulous and tight till he is satisfied;
The wet of woods through the early hours,
Two sleepers at night lying close together as they sleep, one
     with an arm slanting down across and below the waist of
     the other,
The smell of apples, aromas from crush'd sage-plant, mint,
     birch-bark,
The boy's longings, the glow and pressure as he confides to
     me what he was dreaming,
The dead leaf whirling its spiral whirl and falling still and
     content to the ground,
The no-form'd stings that sights, people, objects, sting me
     with,
The hubb'd sting of myself, stinging me as much as it ever
     can any one,
The sensitive, orbic, underlapp'd brothers, that only
     privileged feelers may be intimate where they are,
The curious roamer the hand roaming all over the body, the
     bashful withdrawing of flesh where the fingers
     soothingly pause and edge themselves,
The limpid liquid within the young man,
The vex'd corrosion so pensive and so painful,
The torment, the irritable tide that will not be at rest,
The like of the same I feel, the like of the same in others,
The young man that flushes and flushes, and the young
     woman that flushes and flushes,

The young man that wakes deep at night, the hot hand
    seeking to repress what would master him,
The mystic amorous night, the strange half-welcome pangs,
    visions, sweats,
The pulse pounding through palms and trembling encircling
    fingers, the young man all color'd, red, ashamed, angry;
The souse upon me of my lover the sea, as I lie willing and
    naked,
The merriment of the twin babes that crawl over the grass in
    the sun, the mother never turning her vigilant eyes from
    them,
The walnut-trunk, the walnut-husks, and the ripening or
    ripen'd long-round walnuts,
The continence of vegetables, birds, animals,
The consequent meanness of me should I skulk or find
    myself indecent, while birds and animals never once
    skulk or find themselves indecent,
The great chastity of paternity, to match the great chastity of
    maternity,
The oath of procreation I have sworn, my Adamic and fresh
    daughters,
The greed that eats me day and night with hungry gnaw, till I
    saturate what shall produce boys to fill my place when I
    am through,
The wholesome relief, repose, content,
And this bunch pluck'd at random from myself,
It has done its work—I toss it carelessly to fall where it may.

 1860

FROM PENT-UP
ACHING RIVERS.

From pent-up aching rivers,
From that of myself without which I were nothing,
From what I am determin'd to make illustrious, even if I
    stand sole among men,
From my own voice resonant, singing the phallus,
Singing the song of procreation,
Singing the need of superb children and therein superb
    grown people,
Singing the muscular urge and the blending,
Singing the bedfellow's song, (O resistless yearning!
O for any and each the body correlative attracting!
O for you whoever you are your correlative body! O it, more
    than all else, you delighting!)
From the hungry gnaw that eats me night and day,
From native moments, from bashful pains, singing them,
Seeking something yet unfound though I have diligently
    sought it many a long year.
Singing the true song of the soul fitful at random,
Renascent with grossest Nature or among animals,
Of that, of them and what goes with them my poems
    informing,
Of the smell of apples and lemons, of the pairing of birds,
Of the wet of woods, of the lapping of waves,

Of the mad pushes of waves upon the land, I them chanting,
The overture lightly sounding, the strain anticipating,
The welcome nearness, the sight of the perfect body,
The swimmer swimming naked in the bath, or motionless on
    his back lying and floating,
The female form approaching, I pensive, love-flesh
    tremulous aching,
The divine list for myself or you or for any one making,
The face, the limbs, the index from head to foot, and what it
    arouses,
The mystic deliria, the madness amorous, the utter
    abandonment,
(Hark close and still what I now whisper to you,
I love you, O you entirely possess me,
O that you and I escape from the rest and go utterly off, free
    and lawless,
Two hawks in the air, two fishes swimming in the sea not
    more lawless than we;)
The furious storm through me careering, I passionately
    trembling.
The oath of the inseparableness of two together, of the
    woman that loves me and whom I love more than my life,
    that oath swearing,
(O I willingly stake all for you,
O let me be lost if it must be so!
O you and I! what is it to us what the rest do or think?
What is all else to us? only that we enjoy each other and
    exhaust each other if it must be so;)
From the master, the pilot I yield the vessel to,
The general commanding me, commanding all, from him
    permission taking,

From time the programme hastening, (I have loiter'd too long
  as it is.)
From sex, from the warp and from the woof,
From privacy, from frequent repinings alone,
From plenty of persons near and yet the right person not
  near,
From the soft sliding of hands over me and thrusting of
  fingers through my hair and beard,
From the long sustain'd kiss upon the mouth or bosom,
From the close pressure that makes me or any man drunk,
  fainting with excess,
From what the divine husband knows, from the work of
  fatherhood,
From exultation, victory and relief, from the bedfellow's
  embrace in the night,
From the act-poems of eyes, hands, hips and bosoms,
From the cling of the trembling arm,
From the bending curve and the clinch,
From side by side the pliant coverlet off-throwing,
From the one so unwilling to have me leave, and me just as
  unwilling to leave,
(Yet a moment O tender waiter, and I return,)
From the hour of shining stars and dropping dews,
From the night a moment I emerging flitting out,
Celebrate you act divine and you children prepared for,
And you stalwart loins.

CALAMUS

IN PATHS UNTRODDEN.

In paths untrodden,
In the growth by margins of pond-waters,
Escaped from the life that exhibits itself,
From all the standards hitherto publish'd, from the pleasures,
    profits, conformities,
Which too long I was offering to feed my soul,
Clear to me now standards not yet publish'd, clear to me that
    my soul,
That the soul of the man I speak for rejoices in comrades,
Here by myself away from the clank of the world,
Tallying and talk'd to here by tongues aromatic,
No longer abash'd (for in this secluded spot I can respond as
    I would not dare elsewhere,)
Strong upon me the life that does not exhibit itself, yet
    contains all the rest,
Resolv'd to sing no songs to-day but those of manly
    attachment,
Projecting them along that substantial life,
Bequeathing hence types of athletic love,
Afternoon this delicious Ninth-month in my forty-first year,
I proceed for all who are or have been young men,
To tell the secret of my nights and days,
To celebrate the need of comrades.

WHOEVER YOU ARE HOLDING ME NOW IN HAND.

Whoever you are holding me now in hand,
Without one thing all will be useless,
I give you fair warning before you attempt me further,
I am not what you supposed, but far different.

Who is he that would become my follower?
Who would sign himself a candidate for my affections?

The way is suspicious, the result uncertain, perhaps
    destructive,
You would have to give up all else, I alone would expect to be
    your sole and exclusive standard,
Your novitiate would even then be long and exhausting,
The whole past theory of your life and all conformity to the
    lives around you would have to be abandon'd,
Therefore release me now before troubling yourself any
    further, let go your hand from my shoulders,
Put me down and depart on your way.

Or else by stealth in some wood for trial,
Or back of a rock in the open air,
(For in any roof'd room of a house I emerge not, nor in company,
And in libraries I lie as one dumb, a gawk, or unborn, or dead,)
But just possibly with you on a high hill, first watching lest
    any person for miles around approach unawares,
Or possibly with you sailing at sea, or on the beach of the sea
    of some quiet island,
Here to put your lips upon mine I permit you,

With the comrade's long-dwelling kiss or the new husband's
    kiss,
For I am the new husband and I am the comrade.

Or if you will, thrusting me beneath your clothing,
Where I may feel the throbs of your heart or rest upon your
    hip,
Carry me when you go forth over land or sea;
For thus merely touching you is enough, is best,
And thus touching you would I silently sleep and be carried
    eternally.

But these leaves conning you con at peril,
For these leaves and me you will not understand,
They will elude you at first and still more afterward, I will
    certainly elude you,
Even while you should think you had unquestionably caught
    me, behold!
Already you see I have escaped from you.

For it is not for what I have put into it that I have written this
    book,
Nor is by reading it you will acquire it,
Nor do those know me best who admire me and vauntingly
    praise me,
Nor will the candidates for my love (unless at most a very
    few) prove victorious,
Nor will my poems do good only, they will do just as much
    evil, perhaps more,
For all is useless without that which you may guess at many
    times and not hit, that which I hinted at;
Therefore release me and depart on your way.

FOR YOU O DEMOCRACY.

Come, I will make the continent indissoluble,
I will make the most splendid race the sun ever shone
    upon,
I will make divine magnetic lands,
       With the love of comrades,
          With the life-long love of comrades.

I will plant companionship thick as trees along all the rivers
    of America, and along the shores of the great lakes, and
    all over the prairies,
I will make inseparable cities with their arms about each
    other's necks,
       By the love of comrades,
         By the manly love of comrades.

For you these from me, O Democracy, to serve you ma
    femme!
For you, for you I am trilling these songs.

CITY OF ORGIES.

City of orgies, walks and joys,
City whom that I have lived and sung in your midst will one
    day make you illustrious,
Not the pageants of you, not your shifting tableaus, your
    spectacles, repay me,

Not the interminable rows of your houses, nor the ships at
    the wharves,
Nor the processions in the streets, nor the bright windows
    with goods in them,
Nor to converse with learn'd persons, or bear my share in the
    soiree or feast;
Not those, but as I pass O Manhattan, your frequent and
    swift flash of eyes offering me love,
Offering response to my own—these repay me,
Lovers, continual lovers, only repay me.

TO A STRANGER.

Passing stranger! you do not know how longingly I look upon
    you,
You must be he I was seeking, or she I was seeking, (it comes
    to me as of a dream,)
I have somewhere surely lived a life of joy with you,
All is recall'd as we flit by each other, fluid, affectionate,
    chaste, matured,
You grew up with me, were a boy with me or a girl with me,
I ate with you and slept with you, your body has become not
    yours only nor left my body mine only,
You give me the pleasure of your eyes, face, flesh, as we pass,
    you take of my beard, breast, hands, in return,
I am not to speak to you, I am to think of you when I sit alone
    or wake at night alone,
I am to wait, I do not doubt I am to meet you again,
I am to see to it that I do not lose you.

AMONG THE MULTITUDE.

Among the men and women the multitude,
I perceive one picking me out by secret and divine signs,
Acknowledging none else, not parent, wife, husband, brother,
    child, any nearer than I am,
Some are baffled, but that one is not—that one knows me.

Ah lover and perfect equal,
I meant that you should discover me so by faint indirections,
And I when I meet you mean to discover you by the like in
    you.

TO A COMMON PROSTITUTE.

Be composed—be at ease with me—I am Walt Whitman,
 liberal and lusty as Nature,
Not till the sun excludes you do I exclude you,
Not till the waters refuse to glisten for you and the leaves to
 rustle for you, do my words refuse to glisten and rustle
 for you.
My girl I appoint with you an appointment, and I charge you
 that you make preparation to be worthy to meet me,
And I charge you that you be patient and perfect till I come.

Till then I salute you with a significant look that you do not
 forget me.

MANNAHATTA.

I was asking for something specific and perfect for my city,
Whereupon lo! upsprang the aboriginal name.

Now I see what there is in a name, a word, liquid, sane,
    unruly, musical, self-sufficient,
I see that the word of my city is that word from of old,
Because I see that word nested in nests of water-bays,
    superb,
Rich, hemm'd thick all around with sailships and steamships,
    an island sixteen miles long, solid-founded,
Numberless crowded streets, high growths of iron, slender,
    strong, light, splendidly uprising toward clear skies,
Tides swift and ample, well-loved by me, toward sundown,
The flowing sea-currents, the little islands, larger adjoining
    islands, the heights, the villas,
The countless masts, the white shore-steamers, the lighters,
    the ferry-boats, the black sea-steamers well-model'd,
The down-town streets, the jobbers' houses of business, the
    houses of business of the ship-merchants and money-
    brokers, the river-streets,
Immigrants arriving, fifteen or twenty thousand a week,
The carts hauling goods, the manly race of drivers of horses,
    the brown-faced sailors,

The summer air, the bright sun shining, and the sailing
    clouds aloft,
The winter snows, the sleigh-bells, the broken ice in the
    river, passing along up or down with the flood-tide or
    ebb-tide,
The mechanics of the city, the masters, well-form'd,
    beautiful-faced, looking you straight in the eyes,
Trottoirs throng'd, vehicles, Broadway, the women, the shops
    and shows,
A million people—manners free and superb—open voices—
    hospitality—the most courageous and friendly young
    men,
City of hurried and sparkling waters! city of spires and
    masts!
City nested in bays! my city!

🌿🌿 1865-66 🌿🌿

DRUM-TAPS
[1865]

AND

SEQUEL TO DRUM-TAPS
[1865-66]

VIGIL STRANGE I KEPT ON
THE FIELD ONE NIGHT.

Vigil strange I kept on the field one night;

When you my son and my comrade dropt at my side that day,

One look I but gave which your dear eyes return'd with a
    look I shall never forget,

One touch of your hand to mine O boy, reach'd up as you lay
    on the ground,

Then onward I sped in the battle, the even-contested battle,

Till late in the night reliev'd to the place at last again I made
    my way,

Found you in death so cold dear comrade, found your body
    son of responding kisses, (never again on earth
    responding,)

Bared your face in the starlight, curious the scene, cool blew
    the moderate night-wind,

Long there and then in vigil I stood, dimly around me the
   battle-field spreading,
Vigil wondrous and vigil sweet there in the fragrant silent night,
But not a tear fell, not even a long-drawn sigh, long, long I
   gazed,
Then on the earth partially reclining sat by your side leaning
   my chin in my hands,
Passing sweet hours, immortal and mystic hours with you
   dearest comrade—not a tear, not a word,
Vigil of silence, love and death, vigil for you my son and my
   soldier,
As onward silently stars aloft, eastward new ones upward stole,
Vigil final for you brave boy, (I could not save you, swift was
   your death,
I faithfully loved you and cared for you living, I think we
   shall surely meet again,)
Till at latest lingering of the night, indeed just as the dawn
   appear'd,
My comrade I wrapt in his blanket, envelop'd well his form,
Folded the blanket well, tucking it carefully over head and
   carefully under feet,
And there and then and bathed by the rising sun, my son in
   his grave, in his rude-dug grave I deposited,
Ending my vigil strange with that, vigil of night and battle-
   field dim,
Vigil for boy of responding kisses, (never again on earth
   responding,)
Vigil for comrade swiftly slain, I never forget, how as day
   brighten'd,
I rose from the chill ground and folded my soldier well in his
   blanket,
And buried him where he fell.

THE WOUND-DRESSER.

1

An old man bending I come among new faces,
Years looking backward resuming in answer to
    children,
Come tell us old man, as from young men and maidens that
    love me,
(Arous'd and angry, I'd thought to beat the alarum, and urge
    relentless war,
But soon my fingers fail'd me, my face droop'd and I resign'd
    myself,
To sit by the wounded and soothe them, or silently watch the
    dead;)
Years hence of these scenes, of these furious passions, these
    chances,
Of unsurpass'd heroes, (was one side so brave? the other was
    equally brave;)
Now be witness again, paint the mightiest armies of earth,
Of those armies so rapid so wondrous what saw you to tell
    us?
What stays with you latest and deepest? of curious panics,
Of hard-fought engagements or sieges tremendous what
    deepest remains?

2

O maidens and young men I love and that love me,
What you ask of my days those the strangest and sudden
    your talking recalls,
Soldier alert I arrive after a long march cover'd with sweat
    and dust,

In the nick of time I come, plunge in the fight, loudly shout in
    the rush of successful charge,
Enter the captur'd works—yet lo, like a swift-running river
    they fade,
Pass and are gone they fade—I dwell not on soldiers' perils
    or soldiers' joys,
(Both I remember well—many the hardships, few the joys,
    yet I was content.)

But in silence, in dreams' projections,
While the world of gain and appearance and mirth goes on,
So soon what is over forgotten, and waves wash the imprints
    off the sand,
With hinged knees returning I enter the doors, (while for you
    up there,
Whoever you are, follow without noise and be of strong heart.)

Bearing the bandages, water and sponge,
Straight and swift to my wounded I go,
Where they lie on the ground after the battle brought in,
Where their priceless blood reddens the grass the ground,
Or to the rows of the hospital tent, or under the roof'd hospital,
To the long rows of cots up and down each side I return,
To each and all one after another I draw near, not one do I
    miss,
An attendant follows holding a tray, he carries a refuse pail,
Soon to be fill'd with clotted rags and blood, emptied, and
    fill'd again.

I onward go, I stop,
With hinged knees and steady hand to dress wounds,
I am firm with each, the pangs are sharp yet unavoidable,

One turns to me his appealing eyes—poor boy! I never knew
    you,
Yet I think I could not refuse this moment to die for you, if
    that would save you.

3

On, on I go, (open doors of time! open hospital doors!)
The crush'd head I dress, (poor crazed hand tear not the
    bandage away,)
The neck of the cavalry-man with the bullet through and
    through I examine,
Hard the breathing rattles, quite glazed already the eye, yet
    life struggles hard,
(Come sweet death! be persuaded O beautiful death!
In mercy come quickly.)

From the stump of the arm, the amputated hand,
I undo the clotted lint, remove the slough, wash off the
    matter and blood,
Back on his pillow the soldier bends with curv'd neck and
    side falling head,
His eyes are closed, his face is pale, he dares not look on the
    bloody stump,
And has not yet look'd on it.

I dress a wound in the side, deep, deep,
But a day or two more, for see the frame all wasted and sinking,
And the yellow-blue countenance see.

I dress the perforated shoulder, the foot with the bullet-wound,
Cleanse the one with a gnawing and putrid gangrene, so
    sickening, so offensive,

While the attendant stands behind aside me holding the tray
    and pail.

I am faithful, I do not give out,
The fractur'd thigh, the knee, the wound in the abdomen,
These and more I dress with impassive hand, (yet deep in
    my breast a fire, a burning flame.)

4

Thus in silence in dreams' projections,
Returning, resuming, I thread my way through the hospitals,
The hurt and wounded I pacify with soothing hand,
I sit by the restless all the dark night, some are so young,
Some suffer so much, I recall the experience sweet and sad,
(Many a soldier's loving arms about this neck have cross'd
    and rested,
Many a soldier's kiss dwells on these bearded lips.)

WHEN LILACS LAST IN
THE DOORYARD BLOOM'D.

1

When lilacs last in the dooryard bloom'd,
And the great star early droop'd in the western sky in the
    night,
I mourn'd, and yet shall mourn with ever-returning spring.

Ever-returning spring, trinity sure to me you bring,
Lilac blooming perennial and drooping star in the west,
And thought of him I love.

2

O powerful western fallen star!

O shades of night—O moody, tearful night!

O great star disappear'd—O the black murk that hides the
   star!

O cruel hands that hold me powerless—O helpless soul of me!

O harsh surrounding cloud that will not free my soul.

3

In the dooryard fronting an old farm-house near the white-
   wash'd palings,

Stands the lilac-bush tall-growing with heart-shaped leaves
   of rich green,

With many a pointed blossom rising delicate, with the
   perfume strong I love,

With every leaf a miracle—and from this bush in the
   dooryard,

With delicate-color'd blossoms and heart-shaped leaves of
   rich green,

A sprig with its flower I break.

4

In the swamp in secluded recesses,

A shy and hidden bird is warbling a song.

Solitary the thrush,

The hermit withdrawn to himself, avoiding the settlements,

Sings by himself a song.

Song of the bleeding throat,

Death's outlet song of life, (for well dear brother I know,

If thou wast not granted to sing thou would'st surely die.)

5

Over the breast of the spring, the land, amid cities,
Amid lanes and through old woods, where lately the
    violets peep'd from the ground, spotting the gray
    debris,
Amid the grass in the fields each side of the lanes, passing
    the endless grass,
Passing the yellow-spear'd wheat, every grain from its
    shroud in the dark-brown fields uprisen,
Passing the apple-tree blows of white and pink in the
    orchards,
Carrying a corpse to where it shall rest in the grave,
Night and day journeys a coffin.

6

Coffin that passes through lanes and streets,
Through day and night with the great cloud darkening the
    land,
With the pomp of the inloop'd flags with the cities draped in
    black,
With the show of the States themselves as of crape-veil'd
    women standing,
With processions long and winding and the flambeaus of the
    night,
With the countless torches lit, with the silent sea of faces and
    the unbared heads,
With the waiting depot, the arriving coffin, and the sombre
    faces,
With dirges through the night, with the thousand voices
    rising strong and solemn,
With all the mournful voices of the dirges pour'd around the
    coffin,

The dim-lit churches and the shuddering organs—where
    amid these you journey,
With the tolling tolling bells' perpetual clang,
Here, coffin that slowly passes,
I give you my sprig of lilac.

7

(Nor for you, for one alone,
Blossoms and branches green to coffins all I bring,
For fresh as the morning, thus would I chant a song for you
    O sane and sacred death.

All over bouquets of roses,
O death, I cover you over with roses and early lilies,
But mostly and now the lilac that blooms the first,
Copious I break, I break the sprigs from the bushes,
With loaded arms I come, pouring for you,
For you and the coffins all of you O death.)

8

O western orb sailing the heaven,
Now I know what you must have meant as a month since I
    walk'd,
As I walk'd in silence the transparent shadowy night,
As I saw you had something to tell as you bent to me night
    after night,
As you droop'd from the sky low down as if to my side, (while
    the other stars all look'd on,)
As we wander'd together the solemn night, (for something I
    know not what kept me from sleep,)
As the night advanced, and I saw on the rim of the west how
    full you were of woe,

As I stood on the rising ground in the breeze in the cool
    transparent night,
As I watch'd where you pass'd and was lost in the netherward
    black of the night,
As my soul in its trouble dissatisfied sank, as where you sad
    orb,
Concluded, dropt in the night, and was gone.

9

Sing on there in the swamp,
O singer bashful and tender, I hear your notes, I hear your
    call,
I hear, I come presently, I understand you,
But a moment I linger, for the lustrous star has detain'd me,
The star my departing comrade holds and detains me.

10

O how shall I warble myself for the dead one there I loved?
And how shall I deck my song for the large sweet soul that
    has gone?
And what shall my perfume be for the grave of him I love?

Sea-winds blown from east and west,
Blown from the Eastern sea and blown from the Western sea,
    till there on the prairies meeting,
These and with these and the breath of my chant,
I'll perfume the grave of him I love.

11

O what shall I hang on the chamber walls?
And what shall the pictures be that I hang on the walls,
To adorn the burial-house of him I love?

Pictures of growing spring and farms and homes,

With the Fourth-month eve at sundown, and the gray smoke
lucid and bright,

With floods of the yellow gold of the gorgeous, indolent,
sinking sun, burning, expanding the air,

With the fresh sweet herbage under foot, and the pale green
leaves of the trees prolific,

In the distance the flowing glaze, the breast of the river, with
a wind-dapple here and there,

With ranging hills on the banks, with many a line against the
sky, and shadows,

And the city at hand with dwellings so dense, and stacks of
chimneys,

And all the scenes of life and the workshops, and the
workmen homeward returning.

12

Lo, body and soul—this land,

My own Manhattan with spires, and the sparkling and
hurrying tides, and the ships,

The varied and ample land, the South and the North in the
light, Ohio's shores and flashing Missouri,

And ever the far-spreading prairies cover'd with grass and
corn.

Lo, the most excellent sun so calm and haughty,

The violet and purple morn with just-felt breezes,

The gentle soft-born measureless light,

The miracle spreading bathing all, the fulfill'd noon,

The coming eve delicious, the welcome night and the
stars,

Over my cities shining all, enveloping man and land.

13

Sing on, sing on you gray-brown bird,
Sing from the swamps, the recesses, pour your chant from
    the bushes,
Limitless out of the dusk, out of the cedars and pines.

Sing on dearest brother, warble your reedy song,
Loud human song, with voice of uttermost woe.

O liquid and free and tender!
O wild and loose to my soul—O wondrous singer!
You only I hear—yet the star holds me, (but will soon depart,)
Yet the lilac with mastering odor holds me.

14

Now while I sat in the day and look'd forth,
In the close of the day with its light and the fields of spring,
    and the farmers preparing their crops,
In the large unconscious scenery of my land with its lakes
    and forests,
In the heavenly aerial beauty, (after the perturb'd winds and
    the storms,)
Under the arching heavens of the afternoon swift passing,
    and the voices of children and women,
The many-moving sea-tides, and I saw the ships how they
    sail'd,
And the summer approaching with richness, and the fields
    all busy with labor,
And the infinite separate houses, how they all went on, each
    with its meals and minutia of daily usages,
And the streets how their throbbings throbb'd, and the cities
    pent—lo, then and there,

Falling upon them all and among them all, enveloping me
    with the rest,
Appear'd the cloud, appear'd the long black trail,
And I knew death, its thought, and the sacred knowledge of
    death.

Then with the knowledge of death as walking one side of me,
And the thought of death close-walking the other side of me,
And I in the middle as with companions, and as holding the
    hands of companions,
I fled forth to the hiding receiving night that talks not,
Down to the shores of the water, the path by the swamp in
    the dimness,
To the solemn shadow cedars and ghostly pines so still.

And the singer so shy to the rest receiv'd me,
The gray-brown bird I know receiv'd us comrades three,
And he sang the carol of death, and a verse for him
    I love.

From deep secluded recesses,
From the fragrant cedars and the ghostly pines so still,
Came the carol of the bird.

And the charm of the carol rapt me,
As I held as if by their hands my comrades in the night,
And the voice of my spirit tallied the song of the bird.

Come lovely and soothing death,
Undulate round the world, serenely arriving, arriving,
In the day, in the night, to all, to each,
Sooner or later delicate death.

Prais'd be the fathomless universe,
For life and joy, and for objects and knowledge curious,
And for love, sweet love—but praise! praise! praise!
For the sure-enwinding arms of cool-enfolding death.

Dark mother always gliding near with soft feet,
Have none chanted for thee a chant of fullest welcome?
Then I chant it for thee, I glorify thee above all,
I bring thee a song that when thou must indeed come, come
        unfalteringly.

Approach strong deliveress,
When it is so, when thou hast taken them I joyously sing the dead,
Lost in the loving floating ocean of thee,
Laved in the flood of thy bliss O death.

From me to thee glad serenades,
Dances for thee I propose saluting thee, adornments and
        feastings for thee,
And the sights of the open landscape and the high-spread sky
        are fitting,
And life and the fields, and the huge and thoughtful night.

The night in silence under many a star,
The ocean shore and the husky whispering wave whose voice I
        know,
And the soul turning to thee O vast and well-veil'd death,
And the body gratefully nestling close to thee.

Over the tree-tops I float thee a song,
Over the rising and sinking waves, over the myriad fields and
        the prairies wide,

Over the dense-pack'd cities all and the teeming wharves and
     ways,
I float this carol with joy, with joy to thee O death.

15

To the tally of my soul,
Loud and strong kept up the gray-brown bird,
With pure deliberate notes spreading filling the night.

Loud in the pines and cedars dim,
Clear in the freshness moist and the swamp-perfume,
And I with my comrades there in the night.

While my sight that was bound in my eyes unclosed,
As to long panoramas of visions.

And I saw askant the armies,
I saw as in noiseless dreams hundreds of battle-flags,
Borne through the smoke of the battles and pierc'd with
     missiles I saw them,
And carried hither and yon through the smoke, and torn and
     bloody,
And at last but a few shreds left on the staffs, (and all in
     silence,)
And the staffs all splinter'd and broken.

I saw battle-corpses, myriads of them,
And the white skeletons of young men, I saw them,
I saw the debris and debris of all the slain soldiers of the war,
But I saw they were not as was thought,
They themselves were fully at rest, they suffer'd not,
The living remain'd and suffer'd, the mother suffer'd,

And the wife and the child and the musing comrade suffer'd,
And the armies that remain'd suffer'd.

16

Passing the visions, passing the night,
Passing, unloosing the hold of my comrades' hands,
Passing the song of the hermit bird and the tallying song of
    my soul,
Victorious song, death's outlet song, yet varying ever-altering
    song,
As low and wailing, yet clear the notes, rising and falling,
    flooding the night,
Sadly sinking and fainting, as warning and warning, and yet
    again bursting with joy,
Covering the earth and filling the spread of the heaven,
As that powerful psalm in the night I heard from recesses,
Passing, I leave thee lilac with heart-shaped leaves,
I leave thee there in the door-yard, blooming, returning with
    spring.

I cease from my song for thee,
From my gaze on thee in the west, fronting the west,
    communing with thee,
O comrade lustrous with silver face in the night.

Yet each to keep and all, retrievements out of the night,
The song, the wondrous chant of the gray-brown bird,
And the tallying chant, the echo arous'd in my soul,
With the lustrous and drooping star with the countenance
    full of woe,
With the holders holding my hand nearing the call of the
    bird,

Comrades mine and I in the midst, and their memory ever to
    keep, for the dead I loved so well,
For the sweetest, wisest soul of all my days and lands—and
    this for his dear sake,
Lilac and star and bird twined with the chant of my soul,
There in the fragrant pines and the cedars dusk and dim.

🌿🌿 1867 🌿🌿

SMALL THE THEME OF MY CHANT.

Small the theme of my Chant, yet the greatest—namely,
   One's-Self—a simple, separate person. That, for the use
   of the New World, I sing.
Man's physiology complete, from top to toe, I sing. Not
   physiognomy alone, nor brain alone, is worthy for the
   Muse;—I say the Form complete is worthier far. The
   Female equally with the Male, I sing.
Nor cease at the theme of One's-Self. I speak the word of the
   modern, the word En-Masse.
My Days I sing, and the Lands—with interstice I knew of
   hapless War.
(O friend, whoe'er you are, at last arriving hither to
   commence, I feel through every leaf the pressure of your
   hand, which I return.
And thus upon our journey, footing the road, and more than
   once, and link'd together let us go.)

A NOISELESS
PATIENT SPIDER.

A noiseless patient spider,
I mark'd where on a little promontory it stood isolated,
Mark'd how to explore the vacant vast surrounding,
It launch'd forth filament, filament, filament, out of itself,
Ever unreeling them, ever tirelessly speeding them.

And you O my soul where you stand,
Surrounded, detached, in measureless oceans of space,
Ceaselessly musing, venturing, throwing, seeking the
     spheres to connect them,
Till the bridge you will need be form'd, till the ductile anchor
     hold,
Till the gossamer thread you fling catch somewhere, O my
     soul.

 1888

AS I SIT
WRITING HERE.

As I sit writing here, sick and grown old,
Not my least burden is that dulness of the years, querilities,
Ungracious glooms, aches, lethargy, constipation, whimpering
    ennui,
May filter in my daily songs.

🌾🌾 1891 🌾🌾

GOOD-BYE MY FANCY!

Good-bye my Fancy!
Farewell dear mate, dear love!
I'm going away, I know not where,
Or to what fortune, or whether I may ever see you again,
So Good-bye my Fancy.

Now for my last—let me look back a moment;
The slower fainter ticking of the clock is in me,
Exit, nightfall, and soon the heart-thud stopping.

Long have we lived, joy'd, caress'd together;
Delightful!—now separation—Good-bye my Fancy.

Yet let me not be too hasty,
Long indeed have we lived, slept, filter'd, become really
    blended into one;
Then if we die we die together, (yes, we'll remain one,)
If we go anywhere we'll go together to meet what happens,
May-be we'll be better off and blither, and learn something,
May-be it is yourself now really ushering me to the true
    songs, (who knows?)
May-be it is you the mortal knob really undoing, turning—so
    now finally,
Good-bye—and hail! my Fancy.

PROSE

PREFACE TO
LEAVES OF GRASS

[1855]

Amerca does not repel the past or what it has produced under its forms or amid other politics or the idea of castes or the old religions .... accepts the lesson with calmness ... is not so impatient as has been supposed that the slough still sticks to opinions and manners and literature while the life which served its requirements has passed into the new life of the new forms ... perceives that the corpse is slowly borne from the eating and sleeping rooms of the house ... perceives that it waits a little while in the door ... that it was fittest for its days ... that its action has descended to the stalwart and wellshaped heir who approaches ... and that he shall be fittest for his days.

The Americans of all nations at any time upon the earth have probably the fullest poetical nature. The United States themselves are essentially the greatest poem. In the history of the earth hitherto the largest and most stirring appear tame and orderly to their ampler largeness and stir. Here at last is something in the doings of man that corresponds with the broadcast doings of the day and night. Here is not merely a nation but a teeming nation of nations. Here is action untied from strings necessarily blind to particulars and details magnificently moving in vast masses. Here is the hospitality which forever indicates heroes .... Here are the roughs and beards and space and ruggedness and nonchalance that the soul loves. Here the performance disdaining the trivial unapproached in the tremendous audacity of its crowds and groupings and the push of its perspective spreads with crampless and flowing breadth and showers its prolific and splendid extravagance. One sees it must indeed own the riches of the summer and winter, and need never be bankrupt while corn grows from the ground or the orchards drop apples or the bays contain fish or men beget children upon women.

Other states indicate themselves in their deputies .... but the genius of the United States is not best or most in its executives or legislatures, nor in its ambassadors or authors or colleges or churches or parlors, nor even in its newspapers or inventors ... but always most in the common people. Their manners speech dress friendships—the freshness and candor of their physiognomy—the picturesque looseness of their carriage ... their deathless attachment to freedom—their aversion to anything indecorous or soft or mean—the practical acknowledgment of the citizens of one state by the citizens of all other states—the fierceness of their roused resentment—their curiosity and welcome of novelty—their self-esteem and wonderful sympathy—their susceptibility to a slight—the air they have of persons who never knew how it felt to stand in the presence of superiors—the fluency of their speech—their delight in music, the sure symptom of manly tenderness and native elegance of soul ... their good temper and openhandedness—the terrible significance of their elections—the President's taking off his hat to them not they to him—these too are unrhymed poetry. It awaits the gigantic and generous treatment worthy of it.

The largeness of nature or the nation were monstrous

without a corresponding largeness and generosity of the spirit
of the citizen. Not nature nor swarming states nor streets and
steamships nor prosperous business nor farms nor capital
nor learning may suffice for the ideal of man ... nor suffice
the poet. No reminiscences may suffice either. A live nation
can always cut a deep mark and can have the best authority
the cheapest ... namely from its own soul. This is the sum of
the profitable uses of individuals or states and of present ac-
tion and grandeur and of the subjects of poets. — As if it were
necessary to trot back generation after generation to the east-
ern records! As if the beauty and sacredness of the demon-
strable must fall behind that of the mythical! As if men do not
make their mark out of any times! As if the opening of the
western continent by discovery and what has transpired since
in North and South America were less than the small threatre
of the antique or the aimless sleepwalking of the middle ages!
The pride of the United States leaves the wealth and finesse
of the cities and all returns of commerce and agriculture and
all the magnitude of geography or shows of exterior victory to
enjoy the breed of fullsized men or one fullsized man uncon-
querable and simple.

The American poets are to enclose old and new for Amer-
ica is the race of races. Of them a bard is to be commensurate
with a people. To him the other continents arrive as contribu-
tions ... he gives them reception for their sake and his own
sake. His spirit responds to his country's spirit .... he incar-
nates its geography and natural life and rivers and lakes. Mis-
sissippi with annual freshets and changing chutes, Missouri
and Columbia and Ohio and Saint Lawrence with the falls and
beautiful masculine Hudson, do not embouchure where they
spend themselves more than they embouchure into him. The
blue breadth over the inland sea of Virginia and Maryland and

the sea off Massachusetts and Maine and over Manhattan bay and over Champlain and Erie and over Ontario and Huron and Michigan and Superior, and over the Texan and Mexican and Floridian and Cuban seas and over the seas off California and Oregon, is not tallied by the blue breadth of the waters below more than the breadth of above and below is tallied by him. When the long Atlantic coast stretches longer and the Pacific coast stretches longer he easily stretches with them north or south. He spans between them also from east to west and reflects what is between them. On him rise solid growths that offset the growths of pine and cedar and hemlock and liveoak and locust and chestnut and cypress and hickory and limetree and cottonwood and tuliptree and cactus and wildvine and tamarind and persimmon . . . . and tangles as tangled as any canebrake or swamp . . . . and forests coated with transparent ice and icicles hanging from the boughs and crackling in the wind . . . . and sides and peaks of mountains . . . . and pasturage sweet and free as savannah or upland or prairie . . . . with flights and songs and screams that answer those of the wildpigeon and highhold and orchard-oriole and coot and surf-duck and redshouldered-hawk and fish-hawk and white-ibis and indian-hen and cat-owl and water-pheasant and qua-bird and pied-sheldrake and blackbird and mockingbird and buzzard and condor and night-heron and eagle. To him the hereditary countenance descends both mother's and father's. To him enter the essences of the real things and past and present events—of the enormous diversity of temperature and agriculture and mines—the tribes of red aborigines—the weatherbeaten vessels entering new ports or making landings on rocky coast—the first settlements north or south—the rapid stature and muscle—the haughty defiance of '76, and the war and peace and formation of the constitution .... the union always surrounded by blatherers and always calm and impregnable—the perpetual coming of immigrants—the wharfhem'd cities and superior marine—the unsurveyed interior—the loghouses and clearings and wild animals and hunters and trappers .... the free commerce—the fisheries and whaling and gold-digging—the endless gestation of new states—the convening of Congress every December, the members duly coming up from all climates and uttermost parts .... the noble character of the young mechanics and of all free American workmen and workwomen .... the general ardor and friendliness and enterprise—the perfect equality of the female with the male .... the large amativeness—the fluid movement of the population—the factories and mercantile life and laborsaving machinery—the Yankee swap—the New-York firemen and the target excursion—the southern plantation life—the character of the northeast and of the northwest and southwest—slavery and the tremulous spreading of hands to protect it, and the stern opposition to it which shall never cease till it ceases or the speaking of tongues and the moving of lips cease. For such the expression of the American poet is to be transcendent and new. It is to be indirect and not direct or descriptive or epic. Its quality goes through these to much more. Let the age and wars of other nations be chanted and their eras and characters be illustrated and that finish the verse. Not so the great psalm of the republic. Here the theme is creative and has vista. Here comes one among the wellbeloved stonecutters and plans with decision and science and sees the solid and beautiful forms of the future where there are now no solid forms.

Of all nations the United States with veins full of poetical stuff most need poets and will doubtless have the greatest and use them the greatest. Their Presidents shall not be their

common referee so much as their poets shall. Of all mankind
the great poet is the equable man. Not in him but off from him
things are grotesque or eccentric or fail of their sanity. Noth-
ing out of its place is good and nothing in its place is bad. He
bestows on every object or quality its fit proportions neither
more nor less. He is the arbiter of the diverse and he is the key.
He is the equalizer of his age and land .... he supplies what
wants supplying and checks what wants checking. If peace is
the routine out of him speaks the spirit of peace, large, rich,
thrifty, building vast and populous cities, encouraging agricul-
ture and the arts and commerce—lighting the study of man,
the soul, immortality—federal, state or municipal govern-
ment, marriage, health, freetrade, intertravel by land and
sea .... nothing too close, nothing too far off ... the stars not
too far off. In war he is the most deadly force of the war. Who
recruits him recruits horse and foot ... he fetches parks of ar-
tillery the best that engineer ever knew. If the time becomes
slothful and heavy he knows how to arouse it ... he can make
every word he speaks draw blood. Whatever stagnates in the
flat of custom or obedience or legislation he never stagnates.
Obedience does not master him, he masters it. High up out
of reach he stands turning a concentrated light ... he turns
the pivot with his finger ... he baffles the swiftest runners as he
stands and easily overtakes and envelops them. The time stray-
ing toward infidelity and confections and persiflage he with-
holds by his steady faith ... he spreads out his dishes ... he
offers the sweet firmfibred meat that grows men and women.
His brain is the ultimate brain. He is no arguer ... he is judg-
ment. He judges not as the judge judges but as the sun falling
around a helpless thing. As he sees the farthest he has the
most faith. His thoughts are the hymns of the praise of things.
In the talk on the soul and eternity and God off of his equal

plane he is silent. He sees eternity less like a play with a pro-
logue and denouement . . . . he sees eternity in men and
women . . . he does not see men and women as dreams or dots.
Faith is the antiseptic of the soul . . . it pervades the common
people and preserves them . . . they never give up believing
and expecting and trusting. There is that indescribable fresh-
ness and unconsciousness about an illiterate person that
humbles and mocks the power of the noblest expressive ge-
nius. The poet sees for a certainty how one not a great artist
may be just as sacred and perfect as the greatest art-
ist. . . . . . The power to destroy or remould is freely used by
him but never the power of attack. What is past is past. If he
does not expose superior models and prove himself by every
step he takes he is not what is wanted. The presence of the
greatest poet conquers . . . not parleying or struggling or any
prepared attempts. Now he has passed that way see after him!
there is not left any vestige of despair or misanthropy or cun-
ning or exclusiveness or the ignominy of a nativity or color or
delusion of hell or the necessity of hell . . . . . and no man
thenceforward shall be degraded for ignorance or weakness
or sin.

The greatest poet hardly knows pettiness or triviality. If he
breathes into any thing that was before thought small it di-
lates with the grandeur and life of the universe. He is a
seer . . . . he is individual . . . he is complete in himself . . . . the
others are as good as he, only he sees it and they do not. He is
not one of the chorus . . . . he does not stop for any regula-
tion . . . he is the president of regulation. What the eyesight
does to the rest he does to the rest. Who knows the curious
mystery of the eyesight? The other senses corroborate them-
selves, but this is removed from any proof but its own and
foreruns the identities of the spiritual world. A single glance

of it mocks all the investigations of man and all the instru-
ments and books of the earth and all reasoning. What is mar-
vellous? what is unlikely? what is impossible or baseless or
vague? after you have once just opened the space of a peach-
pit and given audience to far and near and to the sunset and
had all things enter with electric swiftness softly and duly
without confusion or jostling or jam.

The land and sea, the animals fishes and birds, the sky of
heaven and the orbs, the forests mountains and rivers, are not
small themes . . . but folks expect of the poet to indicate more
than the beauty and dignity which always attach to dumb real
objects . . . . they expect him to indicate the path between real-
ity and their souls. Men and women perceive the beauty well
enough . . probably as well as he. The passionate tenacity of
hunters, woodmen, early risers, cultivators of gardens and or-
chards and fields, the love of healthy women for the manly
form, sea-faring persons, drivers of horses, the passion for
light and the open air, all is an old varied sign of the unfailing
perception of beauty and of a residence of the poetic in out-
door people. They can never be assisted by poets to per-
ceive . . . some may but they never can. The poetic quality is
not marshalled in rhyme or uniformity or abstract addresses
to things nor in melancholy complaints or good precepts, but
is the life of these and much else and is in the soul. The profit
of rhyme is that it drops seeds of a sweeter and more luxuri-
ant rhyme, and of uniformity that it conveys itself into its own
roots in the ground out of sight. The rhyme and uniformity of
perfect poems show the free growth of metrical laws and bud
from them as unerringly and loosely as lilacs or roses on a
bush, and take shapes as compact as the shapes of chestnuts
and oranges and melons and pears, and shed the perfume im-
palpable to form. The fluency and ornaments of the finest

poems or music or orations or recitations are not independent but dependent. All beauty comes from beautiful blood and a beautiful brain. If the greatnesses are in conjunction in a man or woman it is enough .... the fact will prevail through the universe .... but the gaggery and gilt of a million years will not prevail. Who troubles himself about his ornaments or fluency is lost. This is what you shall do: Love the earth and sun and the animals, despise riches, give alms to every one that asks, stand up for the stupid and crazy, devote your income and labor to others, hate tyrants, argue not concerning God, have patience and indulgence toward the people, take off your hat to nothing known or unknown or to any man or number of men, go freely with powerful uneducated persons and with the young and with the mothers of families, read these leaves in the open air every season of every year of your life, re-examine all you have been told at school or church or in any book, dismiss whatever insults your own soul, and your very flesh shall be a great poem and have the richest fluency not only in its words but in the silent lines of its lips and face and between the lashes of your eyes and in every motion and joint of your body........ The poet shall not spend his time in unneeded work. He shall know that the ground is always ready ploughed and manured .... others may not know it but he shall. He shall go directly to the creation. His trust shall master the trust of everything he touches .... and shall master all attachment.

The known universe has one complete lover and that is the greatest poet. He consumes an eternal passion and is indifferent which chance happens and which possible contingency of fortune or misfortune and persuades daily and hourly his delicious pay. What balks or breaks others is fuel for his burning progress to contact and amorous joy. Other

proportions of the reception of pleasure dwindle to nothing to
his proportions. All expected from heaven or from the highest
he is rapport with in the sight of the daybreak or a scene of
the winter woods or the presence of children playing or with
his arm round the neck of a man or woman. His love above all
love has leisure and expanse .... he leaves room ahead of
himself. He is no irresolute or suspicious lover ... he is
sure ... he scorns intervals. His experience and the showers
and thrills are not for nothing. Nothing can jar him .... suffer-
ing and darkness cannot—death and fear cannot. To him com-
plaint and jealousy and envy are corpses buried and rotten in
the earth .... he saw them buried. The sea is not surer of the
shore or the shore of the sea than he is of the fruition of his
love and of all perfection and beauty.

The fruition of beauty is no chance of hit or miss ... it is
inevitable as life .... it is exact and plumb as gravitation. From
the eyesight proceeds another eyesight and from the hearing
proceeds another hearing and from the voice proceeds an-
other voice eternally curious of the harmony of things with
man. To these respond perfections not only in the committees
that were supposed to stand for the rest but in the rest them-
selves just the same. These understand the law of perfection
in masses and floods ... that its finish is to each for itself and
onward from itself ... that it is profuse and impartial ... that
there is not a minute of the light or dark nor an acre of the
earth or sea without it—nor any direction of the sky nor any
trade or employment nor any turn of events. This is the reason
that about the proper expression of beauty there is precision
and balance ... one part does not need to be thrust above an-
other. The best singer is not the one who has the most lithe
and powerful organ ... the pleasure of poems is not in them
that take the handsomest measure and similes and sound.

Without effort and without exposing in the least how it is done the greatest poet brings the spirit of any or all events and passions and scenes and persons some more and some less to bear on your individual character as you hear or read. To do this well is to compete with the laws that pursue and follow time. What is the purpose must surely be there and the clue of it must be there . . . . and the faintest indication is the indication of the best and then becomes the clearest indication. Past and present and future are not disjoined but joined. The greatest poet forms the consistence of what is to be from what has been and is. He drags the dead out of their coffins and stands them again on their feet . . . . he says to the past, Rise and walk before me that I may realize you. He learns the lesson . . . . he places himself where the future becomes present. The greatest poet does not only dazzle his rays over character and scenes and passions . . . he finally ascends and finishes all . . . he exhibits the pinnacles that no man can tell what they are for or what is beyond . . . . he glows a moment on the extremest verge. He is most wonderful in his last half-hidden smile or frown . . . by that flash of the moment of parting the one that sees it shall be encouraged or terrified afterward for many years. The greatest poet does not moralize or make applications of morals . . . he knows the soul. The soul has that measureless pride which consists in never acknowledging any lessons but its own. But it has sympathy as measureless as its pride and the one balances the other and neither can stretch too far while it stretches in company with the other. The inmost secrets of art sleep with the twain. The greatest poet has lain close betwixt both and they are vital in his style and thoughts.

The art of art, the glory of expression and the sunshine of the light of letters is simplicity. Nothing is better than simplic-

ity . . . . nothing can make up for excess or for the lack of defi-
niteness. To carry on the heave of impulse and pierce
intellectual depths and give all subjects their articulations are
powers neither common nor very uncommon. But to speak in
literature with the perfect rectitude and insousiance of the
movements of animals and the unimpeachableness of the
sentiment of trees in the woods and grass by the roadside is
the flawless triumph of art. If you have looked on him who has
achieved it you have looked on one of the masters of the art-
ists of all nations and times. You shall not contemplate the
flight of the graygull over the bay or the mettlesome action of
the blood horse or the tall leaning of sunflowers on their stalk
or the appearance of the sun journeying through heaven or
the appearance of the moon afterward with any more satis-
faction than you shall contemplate him. The greatest poet has
less a marked style and is more the channel of thoughts and
things without increase or diminution, and is the free channel
of himself. He swears to his art, I will not be meddlesome, I
will not have in my writing any elegance or effect or original-
ity to hang in the way between me and the rest like curtains. I
will have nothing hang in the way, not the richest curtains.
What I tell I tell for precisely what it is. Let who may exalt or
startle or fascinate or soothe I will have purposes as health or
heat or snow has and be as regardless of observation. What I
experience or portray shall go from my composition without a
shred of my composition. You shall stand by my side and look
in the mirror with me.

The old red blood and stainless gentility of great poets will
be proved by their unconstraint. A heroic person walks at his
ease through and out of that custom or precedent or authority
that suits him not. Of the traits of the brotherhood of writers
savans musicians inventors and artists nothing is finer than

silent defiance advancing from new free forms. In the need of poems philosophy politics mechanism science behaviour, the craft of art, an appropriate native grand-opera, shipcraft, or any craft, he is greatest forever and forever who contributes the greatest original practical example. The cleanest expression is that which finds no sphere worthy of itself and makes one.

The messages of great poets to each man and woman are, Come to us on equal terms, Only then can you understand us, We are no better than you, What we enclose you enclose, What we enjoy you may enjoy. Did you suppose there could be only one Supreme? We affirm there can be unnumbered Supremes, and that one does not countervail another any more than one eyesight countervails another .. and that men can be good or grand only of the consciousness of their supremacy within them. What do you think is the grandeur of storms and dismemberments and the deadliest battles and wrecks and the wildest fury of the elements and the power of the sea and the motion of nature and of the throes of human desires and dignity and hate and love? It is that something in the soul which says, Rage on, Whirl on, I tread master here and everywhere, Master of the spasms of the sky and of the shatter of the sea, Master of nature and passion and death, And of all terror and all pain.

The American bards shall be marked for generosity and affection and for encouraging competitors .. They shall be kosmos .. without monopoly or secrecy .. glad to pass any thing to any one .. hungry for equals night and day. They shall not be careful of riches and privilege .... they shall be riches and privilege .... they shall perceive who the most affluent man is. The most affluent man is he that confronts all the shows he sees by equivalents out of the stronger wealth of himself. The American bard shall delineate no class of persons nor one or two out of the strata of interests nor love most nor trust most nor the soul most nor the body most .... and not be for the eastern states more than the western or the northern states more than the southern.

Exact science and its practical movements are no checks on the greatest poet but always his encouragement and support. The outset and remembrance are there .. there the arms that lifted him first and brace him best .... there he returns after all his goings and comings. The sailor and traveler .. the anatomist chemist astronomer geologist phrenologist spiritualist mathematician historian and lexicographer are not poets, but they are the lawgivers of poets and their construction underlies the structure of every perfect poem. No matter what rises or is uttered they sent the seed of the conception of it ... of them and by them stand the visible proofs of souls ..... always of their fatherstuff must be begotten the sinewy races of bards. If there shall be love and content between the father and the son and if the greatness of the son is the exuding of the greatness of the father there shall be love between the poet and the man of demonstrable science. In the beauty of poems are the tuft and final applause of science.

Great is the faith of the flush of knowledge and of the investigation of the depths of qualities and things. Cleaving and circling here swells the soul of the poet yet is president of itself always. The depths are fathomless and therefore calm. The innocence and nakedness are resumed ... they are neither modest nor immodest. The whole theory of the special and supernatural and all that was twined with it or educed out of it departs as a dream. What has ever happened .... what happens and whatever may or shall happen, the vital laws enclose all .... they are sufficient for any case and for all cases ... none to be hurried or retarded .... any miracle of affairs or persons inadmissible in the vast clear scheme where every motion and every spear of grass and the frames and spirits of men and women and all that concerns them are unspeakably perfect miracles all referring to all and each distinct and in its place. It is also not consistent with the reality of the soul to admit that there is anything in the known universe more divine than men and women.

Men and women and the earth and all upon it are simply to be taken as they are, and the investigation of their past and present and future shall be unintermitted and shall be done with perfect candor. Upon this basis philosophy speculates ever looking toward the poet, ever regarding the eternal tendencies of all toward happiness never inconsistent with what is clear to the senses and to the soul. For the eternal tendencies of all toward happiness make the only point of sane philosophy. Whatever comprehends less than that . . . whatever is less than the laws of light and of astronomical motion . . . or less than the laws that follow the thief the liar the glutton and the drunkard through his life and doubtless afterward . . . . . . or less than vast stretches of time or the slow formation of density or the patient upheaving of strata—is of no account. Whatever would put God in a poem or system of philosophy as contending against some being or influence is also of no account. Sanity and ensemble characterise the great master . . . spoilt in one principle all is spoilt. The great master has nothing to do with miracles. He sees health for himself in being one of the mass . . . . he sees the hiatus in singular eminence. To the perfect shape comes common ground. To be under the general law is great for that is to correspond with it. The master knows that he is unspeakably great and that all are unspeakably great . . . . that nothing for instance is greater than to conceive children and bring them up well . . . that to be is just as great as to perceive or tell.

In the make of the great masters the idea of political liberty
is indispensible. Liberty takes the adherence of heroes wher-
ever men and women exist . . . . but never takes any adherence
or welcome from the rest more than from poets. They are the
voice and exposition of liberty. They out of ages are worthy the
grand idea . . . . to them it is confided and they must sustain it.
Nothing has precedence of it and nothing can warp or degrade
it. The attitude of great poets is to cheer up slaves and horrify
despots. The turn of their necks, the sound of their feet, the
motions of their wrists, are full of hazard to the one and hope
to the other. Come nigh them awhile and though they neither
speak or advise you shall learn the faithful American lesson.
Liberty is poorly served by men whose good intent is quelled
from one failure or two failures or any number of failures,
or from the casual indifference or ingratitude of the people, or
from the sharp show of the tushes of power, or the bringing to
bear soldiers and cannon or any penal statutes. Liberty relies
upon itself, invites no one, promises nothing, sits in calmness
and light, is positive and composed, and knows no discourage-
ment. The battle rages with many a loud alarm and frequent
advance and retreat . . . . the enemy triumphs . . . . the prison,
the handcuffs, the iron necklace and anklet, the scaffold, gar-
rote and leadballs do their work . . . . the cause is asleep . . . . the
strong throats are choked with their own blood . . . . the young
men drop their eyelashes toward the ground when they pass
each other . . . . and is liberty gone out of that place? No never.
When liberty goes it is not the first to go nor the second or
third to go . . it waits for all the rest to go . . it is the last . . . When
the memories of the old martyrs are faded utterly away . . . . when
the large names of patriots are laughed at in the public halls
from the lips of the orators . . . . when the boys are no more
christened after the same but christened after tyrants and trai-

tors instead . . . . when the laws of the free are grudgingly permitted and laws for informers and bloodmoney are sweet to the taste of the people . . . . when I and you walk abroad upon the earth stung with compassion at the sight of numberless brothers answering our equal friendship and calling no man master—and when we are elated with noble joy at the sight of slaves . . . . when the soul retires in the cool communion of the night and surveys its experience and has much extasy over the word and deed that put back a helpless innocent person into the gripe of the gripers or into any cruel inferiority . . . . when those in all parts of these states who could easier realize the true American character but do not yet—when the swarms of cringers, suckers, doughfaces, lice of politics, planners of sly involutions for their own preferment to city offices or state legislatures or the judiciary or congress or the presidency, obtain a response of love and natural deference from the people whether they get the offices or no . . . . when it is better to be a bound booby and rogue in office at a high salary than the poorest free mechanic or farmer with his hat unmoved from his head and firm eyes and a candid and generous heart . . . . and when servility by town or state or the federal government or any oppression on a large scale or small scale can be tried on without its own punishment following duly after in exact proportion against the smallest chance of escape . . . . or rather when all life and all the souls of men and women are discharged from any part of the earth—then only shall the instinct of liberty be discharged from that part of the earth.

As the attributes of the poets of the kosmos concentre in the real body and soul and in the pleasure of things they possess the superiority of genuineness over all fiction and romance. As they emit themselves facts are showered over with light . . . . the daylight is lit with more volatile light . . . . also the

deep between the setting and rising sun goes deeper many
fold. Each precise object or condition or combination or pro-
cess exhibits a beauty . . . . the multiplication table its—old age
its—the carpenter's trade its—the grand-opera its . . . . the
hugehulled cleanshaped New-York clipper at sea under steam
or full sail gleams with unmatched beauty . . . . the American
circles and large harmonies of government gleam with
theirs . . . . and the commonest definite intentions and actions
with theirs. The poets of the kosmos advance through all in-
terpositions and coverings and turmoils and stratagems to
first principles. They are of use . . . . they dissolve poverty from
its need and riches from its conceit. You large proprietor they
say shall not realize or perceive more than any one else. The
owner of the library is not he who holds a legal title to it hav-
ing bought and paid for it. Any one and every one is owner of
the library who can read the same through all the varieties of
tongues and subjects and styles, and in whom they enter with
ease and take residence and force toward paternity and ma-
ternity, and make supple and powerful and rich and
large. . . . . These American states strong and healthy and
accomplished shall receive no pleasure from violations of
natural models and must not permit them. In paintings or
mouldings or carvings in mineral or wood, or in the illustra-
tions of books or newspapers, or in any comic or tragic prints,
or in the patterns of woven stuffs or any thing to beautify
rooms or furniture or costumes, or to put upon cornices or
monuments or on the prows or sterns of ships, or to put any-
where before the human eye indoors or out, that which dis-
torts honest shapes or which creates unearthly beings or
places or contingencies is a nuisance and revolt. Of the hu-
man form especially it is so great it must never be made
ridiculous. Of ornaments to a work nothing outre can be

allowed .. but those ornaments can be allowed that conform to the perfect facts of the open air and that flow out of the nature of the work and come irrepressibly from it and are necessary to the completion of the work. Most works are most beautiful without ornament... Exaggerations will be revenged in human physiology. Clean and vigorous children are jetted and conceived only in those communities where the models of natural forms are public every day..... Great genius and the people of these states must never be demeaned to romances. As soon as histories are properly told there is no more need of romances.

The great poets are also to be known by the absence in them of tricks and by the justification of perfect personal candor. Then folks echo a new cheap joy and a divine voice leaping from their brains: How beautiful is candor! All faults may be forgiven of him who has perfect candor. Henceforth let no man of us lie, for we have seen that openness wins the inner and outer world and that there is no single exception, and that never since our earth gathered itself in a mass have deceit or subterfuge or prevarication attracted its smallest particle or the faintest tinge of a shade—and that through the enveloping wealth and rank of a state or the whole republic of states a sneak or sly person shall be discovered and despised .... and that the soul has never been once fooled and never can be fooled .... and thrift without the loving nod of the soul is only a foetid puff .... and there never grew up in any of the continents of the globe nor upon any planet or satellite or star, nor upon the asteroids, nor in any part of ethereal space, nor in the midst of density, nor under the fluid wet of the sea, nor in that condition which precedes the birth of babes, nor at any time during the changes of life, nor in that condition that follows what we term death, nor in any stretch of abeyance or action afterward of vitality, nor in any process of formation or reformation anywhere, a being whose instinct hated the truth.

Extreme caution or prudence, the soundest organic health, large hope and comparison and fondness for women and children, large alimentiveness and destructiveness and causality, with a perfect sense of the oneness of nature and the propriety of the same spirit applied to human affairs . . these are called up of the float of the brain of the world to be parts of the greatest poet from his birth out of his mother's womb and from her birth out of her mother's. Caution seldom goes far enough. It has been thought that the prudent citizen was the citizen who applied himself to solid gains and did well for himself and his family and completed a lawful life without debt or crime. The greatest poet sees and admits these economies as he sees the economies of food and sleep, but has higher notions of prudence than to think he gives much when he gives a few slight attentions at the latch of the gate. The premises of the prudence of life are not the hospitality of it or the ripeness and harvest of it. Beyond the independence of a little sum laid aside for burial-money, and of a few clapboards around and shingles overhead on a lot of American soil owned, and the easy dollars that supply the year's plain clothing and meals, the melancholy prudence of the abandonment of such a great being as a man is to the toss and pallor of years of moneymaking with all their scorching days and icy nights and all their stifling deceits and underhanded dodgings, or infinitessimals of parlors, or shameless stuffing while others starve . . and all the loss of the bloom and odor of the earth and of the flowers and atmosphere and of the sea and of the true taste of the women and men you pass or have to do with in youth or middle age, and the issuing sickness and desperate revolt at the close of a life without elevation or naivete, and the ghastly chatter of a death without serenity or majesty, is the great fraud upon modern civilization and forethought, blotching the surface and system which civilization undeniably drafts, and moistening with tears the immense features it spreads and spreads with such velocity before the reached kisses of the soul... Still the right explanation remains to be made about prudence. The prudence of the mere wealth and respectability of the most esteemed life appears too faint for the eye to observe at all when little and large alike drop quietly aside at the thought of the prudence suitable for immortality. What is wisdom that fills the thinness of a year or seventy or eighty years to wisdom spaced out by ages and coming back at a certain time with strong reinforcements and rich presents and the clear faces of wedding-guests as far as you can look in every direction running gaily toward you? Only the soul is of itself .... all else has reference to what ensues. All that a person does or thinks is of consequence. Not a move can a man or woman make that affects him or her in a day or a month or any part of the direct lifetime or the hour of death but the same affects him or her onward afterward through the indirect lifetime. The indirect is always as great and real as the direct. The spirit receives from the body just as much as it gives to the body. Not one name of word or deed .. not of venereal sores or discolorations .. not the privacy of the onanist ... not of the putrid veins of gluttons or rumdrinkers ... not peculation or cunning or betrayal or murder .. no serpentine poison of those that seduce women .. not the foolish yielding of women .. not prostitution .. not of any depravity of young men .. not of the attainment of gain by discreditable means .. not any nastiness of appetite .. nor any harshness of officer to men or judges to prisoners or fathers to sons or sons to fathers or of husbands to wives or bosses to

their boys .. not of greedy looks or malignant wishes ... nor
any of the wiles practised by people upon themselves ... ever
is or ever can be stamped on the programme but it is duly re-
alized and returned, and that returned in further perfor-
mances ... and they returned again. Nor can the push of
charity or personal force ever be any thing else than the pro-
foundest reason, whether it bring arguments to hand or no.
No specification is necessary .. to add or subtract or divide is
in vain. Little or big, learned or unlearned, white or black, le-
gal or illegal, sick or well, from the first inspiration down the
windpipe to the last expiration out of it, all that a male or fe-
male does that is vigorous and benevolent and clean is so
much sure profit to him or her in the unshakable order of the
universe and through the whole scope of it forever. If the sav-
age or felon is wise it is well .... if the greatest poet or savan
is wise it is simply the same .. if the President or chief justice
is wise it is the same ... if the young mechanic or farmer is
wise it is no more or less .. if the prostitute is wise it is no
more nor less. The interest will come round .. all will come
round. All the best actions of war and peace ... all help given
to relatives and strangers and the poor and old and sorrowful
and young children and widows and the sick, and to all
shunned persons .. all furtherance of fugitives and of the es-
cape of slaves .. all the self-denial that stood steady and aloof
on wrecks and saw others take the seats of the boats ... all of-
fering of substance or life for the good old cause, or for a
friend's sake or opinion's sake ... all pains of enthusiasts
scoffed at by their neighbors .. all the vast sweet love and pre-
cious suffering of mothers ... all honest men baffled in strifes
recorded or unrecorded .... all the grandeur and good of the
few ancient nations whose fragments of annals we in-
herit .. and all the good of the hundreds of far mightier and

more ancient nations unknown to us by name or date or loca-
tion . . . . all that was ever manfully begun, whether it suc-
ceeded or no . . . . all that has at any time been well suggested
out of the divine heart of man or by the divinity of his mouth
or by the shaping of his great hands . . and all that is well
thought or done this day on any part of the surface of the
globe . . or on any of the wandering stars or fixed stars by
those there as we are here . . or that is henceforth to be well
thought or done by you whoever you are, or by any one—these
singly and wholly inured at their time and inure now and will
inure always to the identities from which they sprung or shall
spring. . . Did you guess any of them lived only its moment?
The world does not so exist . . no parts palpable or impalpable
so exist . . . no result exists now without being from its long
antecedent result, and that from its antecedent, and so back-
ward without the farthest mentionable spot coming a bit
nearer the beginning than any other spot. . . . . Whatever satis-
fies the soul is truth. The prudence of the greatest poet an-
swers at last the craving and glut of the soul, is not
contemptuous of less ways of prudence if they conform to its
ways, puts off nothing, permits no let-up for its own case or
any case, has no particular sabbath or judgment-day, divides
not the living from the dead or the righteous from the unrigh-
teous, is satisfied with the present, matches every thought or
act by its correlative, knows no possible forgiveness or de-
puted atonement . . knows that the young man who compos-
edly periled his life and lost it has done exceeding well for
himself, while the man who has not periled his life and retains
it to old age in riches and ease has perhaps achieved nothing
for himself worth mentioning . . and that only that person has
no great prudence to learn who has learnt to prefer real long-
lived things, and favors body and soul the same, and perceives

the indirect assuredly following the direct, and what evil or good he does leaping onward and waiting to meet him again — and who in his spirit in any emergency whatever neither hurries or avoids death.

The direct trial of him who would be the greatest poet is today. If he does not flood himself with the immediate age as with vast oceanic tides . . . . . and if he does not attract his own land body and soul to himself and hang on its neck with incomparable love and plunge his semitic muscle into its merits and demerits . . . and if he be not himself the age transfigured . . . . and if to him is not opened the eternity which gives similitude to all periods and locations and processes and animate and inanimate forms, and which is the bond of time, and rises up from its inconceivable vagueness and infiniteness in the swimming shape of today, and is held by the ductile anchors of life, and makes the present spot the passage from what was to what shall be, and commits itself to the representation of this wave of an hour and this one of the sixty beautiful children of the wave — let him merge in the general run and wait his development. . . . . Still the final test of poems or any character or work remains. The prescient poet projects himself centuries ahead and judges performer or performance after the changes of time. Does it live through them? Does it still hold on untired? Will the same style and the direction of genius to similar points be satisfactory now? Has no new discovery in science or arrival at superior planes of thought and judgment and behaviour fixed him or his so that either can be looked down upon? Have the marches of tens and hundreds and thousands of years made willing detours to the right hand and the left hand for his sake? Is he beloved long and long after he is buried? Does the young man think often of him? and the young woman think often of him? and do the middleaged and the old think of him?

A great poem is for ages and ages in common and for all degrees and complexions and all departments and sects and for a woman as much as a man and a man as much as a woman. A great poem is no finish to a man or woman but rather a beginning. Has any one fancied he could sit at last under some due authority and rest satisfied with explanations and realize and be content and full? To no such terminus does the greatest poet bring . . . he brings neither cessation or sheltered fatness and ease. The touch of him tells in action. Whom he takes he takes with firm sure grasp into live regions previously unattained . . . . thenceforward is no rest . . . . they see the space and ineffable sheen that turn the old spots and lights into dead vacuums. The companion of him beholds the birth and progress of stars and learns one of the meanings. Now there shall be a man cohered out of tumult and chaos . . . . the elder encourages the younger and shows him how . . . they two shall launch off fearlessly together till the new world fits an orbit for itself and looks unabashed on the lesser orbits of the stars and sweeps through the ceaseless rings and shall never be quiet again.

There will soon be no more priests. Their work is done. They may wait awhile . . perhaps a generation or two . . dropping off by degrees. A superior breed shall take their place . . . . the gangs of kosmos and prophets en masse shall take their place. A new order shall arise and they shall be the priests of man, and every man shall be his own priest. The churches built under their umbrage shall be the churches of men and women. Through the divinity of themselves shall the kosmos and the new breed of poets be interpreters of men and women and of all events and things. They shall find their inspiration in real objects today, symptoms of the past and future . . . . They shall not deign to defend immortality or God or the perfection of things or liberty or the exquisite beauty and reality of the soul. They shall arise in America and be responded to from the remainder of the earth.

The English language befriends the grand American expression . . . . it is brawny enough and limber and full enough. On the tough stock of a race who through all change of circumstance was never without the idea of political liberty, which is the animus of all liberty, it has attracted the terms of daintier and gayer and subtler and more elegant tongues. It is the powerful language of resistance . . . it is the dialect of common sense. It is the speech of the proud and melancholy races and of all who aspire. It is the chosen tongue to express growth faith self-esteem freedom justice equality friendliness amplitude prudence decision and courage. It is the medium that shall well nigh express the inexpressible.

No great literature nor any like style of behaviour or oratory or social intercourse or household arrangements or public institutions or the treatment by bosses of employed people, nor executive detail or detail of the army or navy, nor spirit of legislation or courts or police or tuition or architecture or songs or amusements or the costumes of young men, can long elude the jealous and passionate instinct of American standards. Whether or no the sign appears from the mouths of the people, it throbs a live interrogation in every freeman's and freewoman's heart after that which passes by or this built to remain. Is it uniform with my country? Are its disposals without ignominious distinctions? Is it for the evergrowing communes of brothers and lovers, large, well-united, proud beyond the old models, generous beyond all models? Is it something grown fresh out of the fields or drawn from the sea for use to me today here? I know that what answers for me an American must answer for any individual or nation that serves for a part of my materials. Does this answer? or is it without reference to universal needs? or sprung of the needs of the less developed society of special ranks? or old needs of pleasure overlaid by modern science and forms? Does this acknowledge liberty with audible and absolute acknowledgement, and set slavery at nought for life and death? Will it help breed one goodshaped and wellhung man, and a woman to be his perfect and independent mate? Does it improve manners? Is it for the nursing of the young of the republic? Does it solve readily with the sweet milk of the nipples of the breasts of the mother of many children? Has it too the old ever-fresh forbearance and impartiality? Does it look with the same love on the last born and on those hardening toward stature, and on the errant, and on those who disdain all strength of assault outside of their own?

The poems distilled from other poems will probably pass away. The coward will surely pass away. The expectation of the vital and great can only be satisfied by the demeanor of the vital and great. The swarms of the polished deprecating and reflectors and the polite float off and leave no remembrance. America prepares with composure and goodwill for the visitors that have sent word. It is not intellect that is to be their warrant and welcome. The talented, the artist, the ingenious, the editor, the statesman, the erudite .. they are not unappreciated .. they fall in their place and do their work. The soul of the nation also does it work. No disguise can pass on it .. no disguise can conceal from it. It rejects none, it permits all. Only toward as good as itself and toward the like of itself will it advance half-way. An individual is as superb as a nation when he has the qualities which make a superb nation. The soul of the largest and wealthiest and proudest nation may well go half-way to meet that of its poets. The signs are effectual. There is no fear of mistake. If the one is true the other is true. The proof of a poet is that his country absorbs him as affectionately as he has absorbed it.

FROM
SPECIMEN DAYS

DOWN AT THE FRONT.

FALMOUTH, VA., *opposite Fredericksburgh, December 21, 1862.* —
Begin my visits among the camp hospitals in the army of the
Potomac. Spend a good part of the day in a large brick man-
sion on the banks of the Rappahannock, used as a hospital
since the battle—seems to have receiv'd only the worst cases.
Out doors, at the foot of a tree, within ten yards of the front of
the house, I notice a heap of amputated feet, legs, arms, hands,
&c., a full load for a one-horse cart. Several dead bodies lie
near, each cover'd with its brown woolen blanket. In the door-
yard, towards the river, are fresh graves, mostly of officers,
their names on pieces of barrel-staves or broken boards, stuck
in the dirt. (Most of these bodies were subsequently taken up
and transported north to their friends.) The large mansion is
quite crowded upstairs and down, everything impromptu, no
system, all bad enough, but I have no doubt the best that can
be done; all the wounds pretty bad, some frightful, the men in
their old clothes, unclean and bloody. Some of the wounded
are rebel soldiers and officers, prisoners. One, a Mississippian,
a captain, hit badly in leg, I talk'd with some time; he ask'd me
for papers, which I gave him. (I saw him three months after-
ward in Washington, with his leg amputated, doing well.) I
went through the rooms, downstairs and up. Some of the men
were dying. I had nothing to give at that visit, but wrote a few

letters to folks home, mothers, &c. Also talk'd to three or four, who seem'd most susceptible to it, and needing it.

A NEW YORK SOLDIER.

This afternoon, July 22d, I have spent a long time with Oscar F. Wilber, company G, 154th New York, low with chronic diarrhœa, and a bad wound also. He asked me to read him a chapter in the New Testament. I complied, and ask'd him what I should read. He said, "Make your own choice." I open'd at the close of one of the first books of the evangelists, and read the chapters describing the latter hours of Christ, and the scenes at the crucifixion. The poor, wasted young man ask'd me to read the following chapter also, how Christ rose again. I read very slowly, for Oscar was feeble. It pleased him very much, yet the tears were in his eyes. He ask'd me if I enjoy'd religion. I said, "Perhaps not, my dear, in the way you mean, and yet, may-be, it is the same thing." He said, "It is my chief reliance." He talk'd of death, and said he did not fear it. I said, "Why, Oscar, don't you think you will get well?" He said, "I may, but it is not probable." He spoke calmly of his condition. The wound was very bad, it discharg'd much. Then the diarrhœa had prostrated him, and I felt that he was even then the same as dying. He behaved very manly and affectionate. The kiss I gave him as I was about leaving he return'd fourfold. He gave me his mother's address, Mrs. Sally D. Wilber, Alleghany post-office, Cattaraugus county, N.Y. I had several such interviews with him. He died a few days after the one just described.

ABRAHAM LINCOLN.

August 12th. —I see the President almost every day, as I hap-
pen to live where he passes to or from his lodgings out of
town. He never sleeps at the White House during the hot sea-
son, but has quarters at a healthy location some three miles
north of the city, the Soldiers' home, a United States military
establishment. I saw him this morning about 8½ coming in to
business, riding on Vermont avenue, near L street. He always
has a company of twenty-five or thirty cavalry, with sabres
drawn and held upright over their shoulders. They say this
guard was against his personal wish, but he let his counselors
have their way. The party makes no great show in uniform or
horses. Mr. Lincoln on the saddle generally rides a good-sized,
easy-going gray horse, is dress'd in plain black, somewhat
rusty and dusty, wears a black stiff hat, and looks about as or-
dinary in attire, &c., as the commonest man. A lieutenant, with
yellow straps, rides at his left, and following behind, two by
two, come the cavalry men, in their yellow-striped jackets.
They are generally going at a slow trot, as that is the pace set
them by the one they wait upon. The sabres and accoutre-
ments clank, and the entirely unornamental *cortège* as it trots
towards Lafayette square arouses no sensation, only some cu-
rious stranger stops and gazes. I see very plainly ABRAHAM
LINCOLN's dark brown face, with the deep-cut lines, the eyes,
always to me with a deep latent sadness in the expression. We
have got so that we exchange bows, and very cordial ones.
Sometimes the President goes and comes in an open ba-
rouche. The cavalry always accompany him, with drawn sa-
bres. Often I notice as he goes out evenings—and sometimes
in the morning, when he returns early—he turns off and halts

at the large and handsome residence of the Secretary of War, on K street, and holds conference there. If in his barouche, I can see from my window he does not alight, but sits in his vehicle, and Mr. Stanton comes out to attend him. Sometimes one of his sons, a boy of ten or twelve, accompanies him, riding at his right on a pony. Earlier in the summer I occasionally saw the President and his wife, toward the latter part of the afternoon, out in a barouche, on a pleasure ride through the city. Mrs. Lincoln was dress'd in complete black, with a long crape veil. The equipage is of the plainest kind, only two horses, and they nothing extra. They pass'd me once very close, and I saw the President in the face fully, as they were moving slowly, and his look, though abstracted, happen'd to be directed steadily in my eye. He bow'd and smiled, but far beneath his smile I noticed well the expression I have alluded to. None of the artists or pictures has caught the deep, though subtle and indirect expression of this man's face. There is something else there. One of the great portrait painters of two or three centuries ago is needed.

SOLDIERS AND TALKS.

Soldiers, soldiers, soldiers, you meet everywhere about the city, often superb-looking men, though invalids dress'd in worn uniforms, and carrying canes or crutches. I often have talks with them, occasionally quite long and interesting. One, for instance, will have been all through the peninsula under McClellan—narrates to me the fights, the marches, the strange, quick changes of that eventful campaign, and gives glimpses of many things untold in any official reports or books or journals. These, indeed, are the things that are genuine and precious. The man was there, has been out two years, has been through a dozen fights, the superfluous flesh of talking is long work'd off him, and he gives me little but the hard meat and sinew. I find it refreshing, these hardy, bright, intuitive, American young men, (experienc'd soldiers with all their youth.) The vocal play and significance moves one more than books. Then there hangs something majestic about a man who has borne his part in battles, especially if he is very quiet regarding it when you desire him to unbosom. I am continually lost at the absence of blowing and blowers among these old-young American militaires. I have found some man or other who has been in every battle since the war began, and have talk'd with them about each one in every part of the United States, and many of the engagements on the rivers and harbors too. I find men here from every State in the Union, without exception. (There are more Southerners, especially border State men, in the Union army than is generally supposed.*) I now doubt whether one can get a fair idea of what this war practically is, or what genuine America is, and her character, without some such experience as this I am having.

---

* Mr. Garfield *(In the House of Representatives, April 15, '79.)* "Do gentlemen know that (leaving out all the border States) there were fifty regiments and seven companies of white men in our army fighting for the Union from the States that went into rebellion? Do they know that from the single State of Kentucky more Union soldiers fought under our flag than Napoleon took into the battle of Waterloo? more than Wellington took with all the allied armies against Napoleon? Do they remember that 186,000 color'd men fought under our flag against the rebellion and for the Union, and that of that number 90,000 were from the States which went into rebellion?"

SPIRITUAL CHARACTERS
AMONG THE SOLDIERS.

Every now and then, in hospital or camp, there are beings I meet—specimens of unworldliness, disinterestedness, and animal purity and heroism—perhaps some unconscious Indianian, or from Ohio or Tennessee—on whose birth the calmness of heaven seems to have descended, and whose gradual growing up, whatever the circumstances of work-life or change, or hardship, or small or no education that attended it, the power of a strange spiritual sweetness, fibre and inward health, have also attended. Something veil'd and abstracted is often a part of the manners of these beings. I have met them, I say, not seldom in the army, in camp, and in the hospitals. The Western regiments contain many of them. They are often young men, obeying the events and occasions about them, marching, soldiering, fighting, foraging, cooking, working on farms or at some trade before the war—unaware of their own nature, (as to that, who is aware of his own nature?) their companions only understanding that they are different from the rest, more silent, "something odd about them," and apt to go off and meditate and muse in solitude.

FROM

MEMORANDA

DURING THE WAR

LETTER TO PARENTS OF
ERASTUS HASKELL

TO MR. AND MRS. S. B. HASKELL

Washington
August 10 1863

Mr and Mrs Haskell,

Dear friends, I thought it would be soothing to you to have a few lines about the last days of your son Erastus Haskell of Company K, 141st New York Volunteers. I write in haste, & nothing of importance—only I thought any thing about Erastus would be welcome. From the time he came to Armory Square Hospital till he died, there was hardly a day but I was with him a portion of the time—if not during the day, then at night. I had no opportunity to do much, or any thing for him, as nothing was needed, only to wait the progress of his malady. I am only a friend, visiting the wounded & sick soldiers, (not connected with any society—or State.) From the first I felt that Erastus was in danger, or at least was much worse than they in the hospital supposed. As he made no complaint, they perhaps [thought him] not very bad—I told the [doctor of the

ward] to look him over again—he was a much [sicker boy?]
than he supposed, but he took it lightly, said, I know more
about these fever cases than you do—the young man looks
very sick, but I shall certainly bring him out of it all right. I
have no doubt the doctor meant well & did his best—at any
rate, about a week or so before Erastus died he got really
alarmed & after that he & all the doctors tried to help him, but
without avail—Maybe it would not have made any difference
any how—I think Erastus was broken down, poor boy, before
he came to the hospital here—I believe he came here about
July 11th—Somehow I took to him, he was a quiet young man,
behaved always correct & decent, said little—I used to sit on
the side of his bed—I said once, You don't talk any, Erastus,
you leave me to do all the talking—he only answered quietly, I
was never much of a talker. The doctor wished every one to
cheer him up very lively—I was always pleasant & cheerful
with him, but did not feel to be very lively—Only once I tried
to tell him some amusing narratives, but after a few moments
I stopt, I saw that the effect was not good, & after that I never
tried it again—I used to sit by the side of his bed, pretty silent,
as that seemed most agreeable to him, & I felt it so too—he
was generally opprest for breath, & with the heat, & I would
fan him—occasionally he would want a drink—some days he
dozed a good deal—sometimes when I would come in, he
woke up, & I would lean down & kiss him, he would reach out
his hand & pat my hair & beard a little, very friendly, as I sat
on the bed & leaned over him.

Much of the time his breathing was hard, his throat
worked—they tried to keep him up by giving him stimulants,
milk-punch, wine &c—these perhaps affected him, for often
his mind wandered somewhat—I would say, Erastus, don't you

remember me, dear son?—can't you call me by name?—once
he looked at me quite a while when I asked him, & he men-
tioned over in[audibly?] a name or two (one sounded like [Mr.
Setchell]) & then, as his eyes closed, he said quite slow, as if to
himself, I don't remember, I dont remember, I dont—it was
quite pitiful—one thing was he could not talk very comfort-
ably at any time, his throat & chest seemed stopped—I have
no doubt at all he had some complaint besides the typhoid—
In my limited talks with him, he told me about his brothers &
sisters by name, & his parents, wished me to write his parents
& send them & all his love—I think he told me about his broth-
ers living in different places, one in New York City, if I recol-
lect right—From what he told me, he must have been poorly
enough for several months before he came to Armory Sq[uare]
Hosp[ital]—the first week in July I think he told me he was
miles from White House, on the peninsula—previous to that,
for quite a long time, although he kept around, he was not at
all well—couldn't do much—was in the band as a fifer I be-
lieve—While he lay sick here he had his fife laying on the lit-
tle stand by his side—he once told me that if he got well he
would play me a tune on it—but, he says, I am not much of a
player yet.

I was very anxious he should be saved, & so were they
all—he was well used by the attendants—poor boy, I can see
him as I write—he was tanned & had a fine head of hair, &
looked good in the face when he first came, & was in pretty
good flesh too—(had his hair cut close about ten or twelve
days before he died)—He never complained—but it looked
pitiful to see him lying there, with such a look out of his eyes.
He had large clear eyes, they seemed to talk better than
words—I assure you I was attracted to him much—Many

nights I sat in the hospital by his bedside till far in the night—
The lights would be put out—yet I would sit there silently,
hours, late, perhaps fanning him—he always liked to have me
sit there, but never cared to talk—I shall never forget those
nights, it was a curious & solemn scene, the sick & wounded
lying around in their cots, just visible in the darkness, & this
dear young man close at hand lying on what proved to be his
death bed—I do not know his past life, but what I do know, &
what I saw of him, he was a noble boy—I felt he was one I
should get very much attached to. I think you have reason to
be proud of such a son, & all his relatives have cause to trea-
sure his memory.

I write you this letter, because I would do something at
least in his memory—his fate was a hard one, to die so—He is
one of the thousands of our unknown American young men in
the ranks about whom there is no record or fame, no fuss
made about their dying so unknown, but I find in them the
real precious & royal ones of this land, giving themselves up,
aye even their young & precious lives, in their country's
cause—Poor dear son, though you were not my son, I felt to
love you as a son, what short time I saw you sick & dying
here—it is as well as it is, perhaps better—for who knows
whether he is not better off, that patient & sweet young soul,
to go, than we are to stay? So farewell, dear boy—it was my
opportunity to be with you in your last rapid days of death—
no chance as I have said to do any thing particular, for nothing
[could be done—only you did not lay] here & die among
strangers without having one at hand who loved you dearly, &
to whom you gave your dying kiss—

Mr. and Mrs. Haskell, I have thus written rapidly whatever
came up about Erastus, & now must close. Though we are

strangers & shall probably never see each other, I send you & all Erastus' brothers and sisters my love—

WALT WHITMAN

I live when home, in Brooklyn, N Y. (in Portland avenue, 4th door north of Myrtle, my mother's residence.) My address here is care of Major Hapgood, paymaster U S A, cor 15th & F st, Washington D C.